STOP BUDGETING

Transform Your Money Mindset, Transform Your Life

START LIVING

LISA CHASTAIN

A SAVIO REPUBLIC BOOK
An Imprint of Post Hill Press
ISBN: 979-8-88845-771-9
ISBN (eBook): 979-8-88845-772-6

Stop Budgeting, Start Living:
Transform Your Money Mindset, Transform Your Life
© 2025 by Millennial Consulting LLC
All Rights Reserved

Cover Design by Jim Villaflores

This book, as well as any other Savio Republic publications, may be purchased in bulk quantities at a special discounted rate. Contact orders@posthillpress.com for more information.

This is a work of nonfiction. All people, locations, events, and situations are portrayed to the best of the author's memory.

No part of this book may be reproduced, stored in a retrieval system, or transmitted by any means without the written permission of the author and publisher.

posthillpress.com
New York • Nashville
Published in the United States of America

1 2 3 4 5 6 7 8 9 10

*To my boys. You are my reason. You are my everything.
Together we are building a world with love. I love you forever.*

TABLE OF CONTENTS

The Beginning 1

PART ONE: THE ROOT

Shame Shame Shame 19
Set Point 29
The Toxicity of Should 37
Staring Fear in the Face 45

PART TWO: OWNERSHIP

Freedom Is on the Other Side of Perfectionism 61
Radical Responsibility 69
Rewrite the Script 83

PART THREE: REDEFINING SUCCESS

Make It Deeply Personal 93
Uncover Your Truth 99
Emotional Bank Account 107
Break the Glass Ceiling 117

PART FOUR: LIVING YOUR HIGHEST PURPOSE

Hell Yes 127
Trusting Yourself with Money 135
Embracing Your Shadow 147
The Journey of Healing 155

PART FIVE: CONSCIOUS REDESIGN

The Stop Budgeting Playbook 165
The End Is the Beginning 187

Appendix: Glossary of Terms 191
References 197
About the Author 199

THE BEGINNING

It's November 15, 1979, at 10 in the morning.

The doctor yells out, "It's a boy!" Tim and Diane are relieved and elated that their family is finally complete. With an almost three-year-old little girl eagerly waiting to be his big sister, their baby boy is born and is finally here. He's six weeks early, five pounds, and healthy. Diane looks at Tim and says, "We are complete."

In 1979, ultrasounds weren't used unless absolutely necessary. Through routine check-ups and sonograms, the heartbeat sounded strong, and they had every reason to believe they were having a healthy baby. They didn't know if it was going to be a boy or a girl, but they were rooting for this kid to be a boy.

Tim is a rough-around-the-edges kind of guy. A former motorcycle racer, he loves the outdoors, and as a stagehand, he can fix just about anything with his hands. His family knows him as the real-life MacGyver, and as much as he loves his little girl, he really wants a boy.

Nervous, excited, and working off a few shots from the bar he was at when he got the call that Diane was in labor, Tim flashes back to the two children he lost after childbirth from his previous marriage. Is it possible that God is so kind to give him another chance to be a father to a girl and a boy? It appears to be so. He's as equally grateful as he is terrified.

As a stagehand since the tender age of seventeen, he's been working so hard. Already on his third marriage, he knows the work it's going to take to make this new family work. He's up to the challenge, and then he hears the doctor say, "Hold on just a second."

The blood rushes out of his body. His face turns pale white. Although exhausted and shaking from delivery, Diane sits up and says, "What is it?"

Dr. Snavely says, with a smile on his face, "There's one more…"

Tim asks, "What do you mean, one more?"

Diane asks, "One more what?"

Dr. Snavely replies, "A baby. You are having twins. Time to push!!"

Four minutes later, a baby girl is born. At four pounds six ounces, she fits in the palm of Tim's hand from head to toe. Another wave of terror rushes over him.

Tim says, "We only planned for one baby. We only have one crib. We had one name picked out. We only have one car seat. There's not enough room. There's not enough. There's not enough."

And the little girl hears her first words from her father and her mother: "This wasn't the plan, and there's not enough."

• • • •

Stop budgeting,
That restaurant is way out of my budget.

I don't think I budgeted enough for my trip—do you mind if we take the train rather than Uber? It's only an extra hour.

Sorry—I totally blew my budget last weekend, so unfortunately I can't pay for a movie ticket.

If you're like most Americans, a phrase like this has probably exited your mouth at one point in the last thirty days. How did it make you feel?

Guilty? Ashamed? Embarrassed? Irresponsible?

The common denominator is that one nauseating word: budget.

From an early age, we're told that a typical budget—with its cookie-cutter worksheet format and restrictive categories—is the key to financial wellness. As we grow up and start managing our own money, we're scorned if we don't have a budget and shamed if we do. Every time we work up our energy to use one, it just ends up discarded alongside all our New Year's resolutions (and then we feel guilty about that, too). At the end of the day, all a budget really does is feed a scarcity beast and limit our ability to freely make our own financial decisions. As long as our finances are in this state, our life is not our own. We stay stuck where we are in our lives and careers because everything we do is based on our finances and not on what we actually want: freedom.

The traditional budget is dead (or at least it should be).

Why did I become a money coach? I needed me when I was younger. Contrary to many other experts today, I didn't grow up around money. I knew nothing about money (and am still navigating the highs and lows of business ownership). I know *exactly* what it feels to feel hopeless and helpless when it comes to money and life. I still journey to those late-night soul sessions at 2 a.m.—a lot less than I used to, but it still happens. I still worry about the state of affairs on our planet. I still worry that a big recession or depression will wipe out our retirement funds. I still worry about my kids, paying bills, my dogs, and my parents. I am far from perfect.

Aren't we all a mess? Aren't we all just trying to figure out what we're doing here on this planet?

In my career, I have worked with hundreds of women who come to me feeling financially illiterate and with a ton of anxiety around numbers. I am profoundly grateful for the work I do every single day. Money and life—they are inextricable. Our money does not just exist in a vacuum; it is the tool that helps us *live* as we desire.

The secret to life is not having billions of dollars. The secret to life is that no one makes it out alive, and no one takes their money with them.

No one is lying on their deathbed saying, "I wish I would have saved more money."

This is the secret to money. Life. Living is the secret to money.

Most people create budgets to control their spending impulses and ideally create more savings. After all, this is what the financial industry has been telling us for years, and as good girls, we want to follow the rules and do things the right way.

The problem is, for so many of us, we then feel like failures if we can't "stick to it" or like there is something wrong with us if it "just doesn't work." For those of us who were born into the "not enough" conversation, we have had to fight like hell to conquer an inherited mindset that does not serve us.

No one has ever given us permission to spend money, and it's causing us all a great deal of pain.

Budgeting does nothing to address the underlying problems with our money mindset. Budgeting only exacerbates the plague of financial inequity. Those who don't have money are ashamed and guilty for spending it. Those who have money are edified for their fortune, and if you're a part of the ever-growing middle and lower class of Americans today, the only thing you've been told is that you're stupid for the choices you're making and that you must budget to better control your spending.

Despite the widespread belief that budgets are the solution, most Americans still live paycheck to paycheck.

Budgets aren't the magical solution — so why does the finance industry keep pretending they are?

Controlling our behavior or attempting to control our behavior only produces results that are more of the same. To transform our lives, we must start with the single most important part of the equation, and that is our mindset. Specifically, our beliefs, our thoughts, where they came from, and how to change them.

If you watch or listen to mainstream media, you'll hear a lot of self-proclaimed financial experts talk about how stupid people are for the choices they make financially.

I'm writing this book because I am sick and tired of hearing people get beat up on, and I'm on a mission to change this industry to something more loving, more healed, and to be perfectly honest, *feminine*.

ABOUT THE AUTHOR

Hi, I'm Lisa. I am the baby girl who surprised the hell out of my parents on the morning of November 15, 1979.

I'm born to a blue-collar family. My family didn't even know they were having me, and life just seemed like there was never enough growing up.

My mom taught us to be grateful for everything. We always had food on the table, and there was always an abundance of family around. I really do have so much to be grateful for. That said, from a very young age, I knew that if I wanted anything in life I was going to have to fight for it, work for it, negotiate for it, and make it happen myself.

That's life in a blue-collar family. You work.

I didn't become a multimillionaire by the time I was ten, and I'm not "self-made"—I've had a lot of support along the way. I don't have it all figured out, and I'm definitely not a manifestation queen. I'm still working on the manifestation thing, I hate budgeting, and I've spent years figuring out how to have a healthy relationship with money. I didn't pay off $700,000 in debt in two days. I've messed up—a lot. I make mistakes, I'm imperfect, and at the age of forty-four, I'm still trying to figure out how to wake up and just be...happy.

My journey with money has been tumultuous, marked by significant highs and lows, and ultimately, incredibly transformative. From a young age, my beliefs about money were shaped by my experiences, leading me to adopt a mindset that there was never enough. By the age of seven, these beliefs had taken root, setting a financial set point that influenced my decisions for years to come.

I was born in Las Vegas to a stagehand dad and a stay-at-home mom. I'm a twin, and my parents thought they were only having one baby until four minutes after my brother was born, when I decided to follow him out of the womb. Things were already tight with my older sister, and the addition of a surprise third child certainly didn't make things any easier. It always seemed like there just wasn't quite enough of anything: our car was too small, house too constricted, and budget too strained. Still, I always had high standards for myself. I was an overachiever—homecoming queen, student body president, tennis captain, prom princess, and top of my class academically. I was addicted to external validation.

Growing up, I expected to be a stay-at-home mom, just like the women around me. But when I got to college, I was introduced to people who *actually* had money. Girls in designer clothing were driving around in their BMWs, and the "you don't have enough" conversation just got louder and louder in my head. I started to overspend on credit cards as a way to try to keep up. And, by the time I was twenty-eight, I had done what good girls are supposed to do: graduate from college, land a job, get married, buy a house, and have a kid.

In 2011, I faced a fork in the road. I had been working at the honors college at the University of Nevada, Las Vegas, in academic advising as the youngest director on campus, and my then husband had skyrocketed up the ranks at Wolfgang Puck to become general manager. He was working eighty- to one-hundred-hour weeks while I worked fifty- to sixty-hour weeks, and it quickly became clear that we couldn't both continue to be away from home that much while also trying to raise a young son. I also recognized that I had maxed out in my role and was looking for a new challenge.

Nine months after I left my career, my husband lost his job (for the first time). He was in and out of work for the remainder of our marriage, and he also began to drink heavily. We were extremely stressed about money, and I knew that I had to go back to work—I just knew I didn't want it to be in higher education.

One day, I got an email from Farmers Insurance saying that I could make $400,000 a year selling insurance. Like with many things, it seemed way too good to be true. Never had I ever thought about selling insurance; no one grows up wanting to be an insurance agent. And, in my family, no one worked in financial services. I had no idea what I would be getting myself into. I didn't really want to go to Farmers and have to work for somebody else, but it did pique my interest in the industry. Unlimited earning potential sounded sexy and foreign. So, I called my best friend and financial adviser and asked if there was really that much money to be had in the space. They weren't kidding, she said, but hey—why didn't I come work for her as a financial adviser?

After extensive research, I made a conscious decision to join her firm and put in sweat equity while I got my necessary licenses and learned the industry. Fast-forward three years, and I was struggling. What I didn't realize at the time of joining my friend's firm is that the finance industry is sink or swim, and I was sinking. I was hustling and learning as quickly as I could, but I just bled money for three years. At the same time, I was trying to keep my marriage intact while maintaining the persona of a calm, confident professional at work. No one knew how badly I was struggling in either my professional or personal life, and I felt extremely isolated and would lie awake at night with stress and anxiety.

Eventually, I was down to my last $20,000 after having drained my 401(k) from $100,000. At the rate that my ex-husband was burning through cash in his addiction, I knew it wasn't going to last. I had to do something.

There was a woman I had been following online who was a coach for financial advisers. Taking a giant risk, I paid her $10,000 and flew to New Jersey to meet with her. I didn't even know if my credit card would go through to pay for the hotel room at that point. Within the first 90 days, I had made $12,000—more money than I had ever earned in that period of time. I left my company and went out on my own as a money coach. In the first ten months, I made six figures.

I created my business to be a counterexample to all the toxic money conversations that are rampant in our society today. Clients can come to me and be honest about saying, "Lisa, I have no idea what the hell I'm doing." Sometimes we don't even talk about money until our second or third meeting. Instead, we focus on what else is happening with their emotions, environments, and patterns that might be contributing to suboptimal money management and life living. I believe strongly that our financial lives are inherently interwoven with our actual lives, and you can't address one without addressing the other.

For the past twenty years, I've worked as an adviser and coach, and I have a passion for coaching—something I'm really good at. In July of 2014, I was thirty-four years old with a six-year-old son, married, and spending a lot of time trying to fix other people, including my ex-husband. Little did I know, my life was about to change forever—and I desperately wanted it to. But I was afraid. Afraid of everything that was about to happen. Afraid of the divorce I knew I needed. Afraid that I was going to lose everything—which I eventually almost did.

I was terrified of what my family, clients, friends, and colleagues would think of me if they knew I was drawing money out of my 401(k) to keep my bills paid and fund a business I had high hopes for, which ultimately failed. Despite the fear, I had a big dream in my heart. So, here's what happened.

Everything changed, and my life course corrected in a way that can only be orchestrated by God. I went through with the divorce. I sold my house. I nearly lost everything. I have been in and out of credit card debt to get out of my marriage, change careers, and start a business. My ex-husband surrendered to addiction and lost everything. My family and I had a falling out (and then we reconciled). I rebounded after my marriage with a childhood friend who turned out to be a bipolar schizophrenic (which was not a lot of fun). I changed career paths. Broke up with my business partner. Made my first six figures ever. Kept my business afloat during COVID. Got remarried. My new husband's ex-wife passed away. My son's dad moved across the country. I adopted my stepson. And through it all, I kept my business going.

And there was a lot in between.

As a financial adviser turned money coach, I have navigated the complexities of personal finance, confronting my own struggles head-on. At thirty-five, I faced a pivotal moment that reshaped my understanding of money, and by thirty-eight, a divorce forced me to reevaluate my financial strategies and mindset. These experiences have underscored the crucial role that our beliefs and attitudes play in achieving financial success.

In this book, I will share my method. You will find my strategies for shifting your own mindset and making savvy financial decisions. It is not just about the numbers; it's about transforming your relationship with money and your life. Together, we will explore the importance of financial emotional intelligence (EQ), providing you with the tools to alleviate shame and fear and embrace a healthier financial life.

We will begin by examining our own feelings and beliefs about money and their origins. Understanding how our mindset acts as a financial set point is essential for making positive changes. Before you can influence others, it's vital to apply these lessons to yourself. This book will guide you in identifying your own talents and superpowers so that you can develop confidence and heal from any guilt or shame that you've experienced in your life as it pertains to money.

Recognizing and reframing limiting beliefs formed in childhood is a significant step toward financial health. By addressing your deep-seated perceptions and beliefs, you can unlock our unique pathway to wealth, and define what freedom means to you. This journey is profoundly personal, and it requires introspection and commitment, but the rewards are life altering.

Today, my life is good. And there is no magic. I work. I write. I love. I try. I mess up. I make mistakes. And with all of my work and discoveries, I consistently remind myself to be fucking grateful. For everything.

Join me as we delve into the intersection of personal finance and mindset, uncovering the secrets to overcoming obstacles and creating a life that you love to live. Together, we will reimagine our relationship with money, paving the way for a future defined by abundance and confidence.

PART ONE
THE ROOT

• • • •

No one comes from earth like grass.
We come like trees. We all have roots.
—*Maya Angelou*

"Be a good girl"
   "Be perfect"
   "Don't rock the boat"
   "Smile"
   "Get straight A's"
   "Be skinny"

Rules. I hate rules. In my household, some were unspoken, and some were said as passive-aggressive comments. The formula was clear. Be a good girl, be polite, and as long as you're not bothering anyone, you're free to do what you want. Unless it isn't what we want for you. Then, if you do anything we don't agree with, you're out.

Control. Women have been controlled from the moment of conception. Told what to do with our bodies, how to act, what to say, how to behave, and if we don't do what we are told to do, then we are failures, shunned, shut out, scorned, and left out.

This is a common experience for women across the planet, from the beginning of time.

And when it comes to our money, the narrative is the same.

Self-control, discipline, sacrifice, cut back, and budget.

Don't dream, don't think big, you're crazy if you think you're anything but destined to have babies and live under someone's shameful cloud of control.

Women globally are increasing their financial firepower. A 2024 article on Equities.com notes that "about 33% of the world's wealth was held by women in 2022, about half of that held by U.S. women."

Women spend more time than men *making economic decisions* for their families, including consumer goods and services. In the U.S. women control or influence 85% of consumer spending. This widely cited statistic is commonly attributed to market research studies and reports by organizations such as Nielsen, Deloitte, and Boston Consulting Group (BCG).

We don't own most of the wealth, but we spend most of it.

We have little ownership, and yet we have all of the control, which makes our relationship with money insanely complicated. We make less, we spend most, and there is no rule book or authority on how we could ever change this for the better.

This is exactly the question I'm asking now, at the moment I write this. How do we change this? And where do we start?

I did what "good middle-class girls" do in America. I went to college, worked three jobs, got a good, safe government job out of college, got married, bought a house, and had a kid all by the age of twenty-eight. Underlying all of that, I numbed out. I kept my head down, I didn't rock the boat, and I became addicted to external validation. I climbed the corporate ladder, I worked sixty hours a week. I ignored the fact that my husband (now ex-husband) drank himself to sleep on the couch every night. If he wasn't home watching TV and drinking, he was working. It was a vicious cycle. I am not proud of it. I was skin and bones, I was stressed out, and there was no end in sight. My only "relief" was the occasional girls trip or girls night out only to be greeted by my toddler at 5:30 a.m.—and I did it all. over. again.

There was no Instagram then. And if there was, I am sure I would have drowned myself in comparison with other moms who "had their shit together"—as if I wasn't comparing myself enough to the other women out there who seemed to be crushing it.

I was doing good work. I was making a difference for others. I was the one losing.

In addition to being emotionally disconnected from my husband (or anyone for that matter), I thought I was taking all of the "right steps." I had saved in my 401(k) like a "good girl." I was giving myself away in every aspect of my life. I showed up every day for a job that I loved. My job as an academic adviser was my sanctuary. I could go to work and be validated. I loved my boss, I loved the students I was advising, and I could go there and *not* feel like I was fucking up my life. On the outside looking in, I probably looked like I had it all together. A 1.5-carat diamond ring on my finger, a beautiful two-story house in an upscale neighborhood, two cars, a husband working at a nationally recognized and celebrated restaurant, a healthy child, designer clothing, and even a Rolex.

At thirty-one, after a decade of this masquerade, raising my demanding toddler, I hit a wall. I was being questioned at work for not having the credentials I needed to excel in my career, and impostor syndrome was screaming in my ears. All of the things collided: my absent husband; living far enough away from family and not feeling like I could ask for help; our financial responsibilities; and running a household. I folded under the pressure of my life. I made up my mind that something had to give. Someone between my husband and I had to make a change for my son's sake. So, I did what so many women have done in the history of time.

I took a step back, "for my family."

Never mind the fact that I loved my job. Never mind the fact that I was really good at being an adviser. Why was it that I had to fall on the metaphorical sword of leaving my career behind to take care of my family? What I realized years later is that *I didn't value myself.* And, as a woman in America, it was the acceptable thing to do. And *that* was the reason for my meltdown. Because I didn't value myself, I was a doormat in relationships, financially and emotionally. I was giving and giving and giving at the sake of my own mental health, and I folded. Honestly, it felt like an implosion.

I left my job in 2011 and everything changed.

SHAME SHAME SHAME

"If you want to own a house one day, stop buying avocado toast and lattes."

"You have credit card debt? Oof, that's rough. You must have made some pretty irresponsible decisions."

"I don't know why she thinks she needs designer clothes. We all know she doesn't make enough money to afford them."

In today's society, there is *so* much judgment around money (and righteousness around budgeting). Some of it comes from other people, and much is self-inflicted.

Where does the shame come from?

Brené Brown provides a clear definition of shame in her book *Daring Greatly*. She writes:

"Shame is the intensely painful feeling or experience of believing that we are flawed and therefore unworthy of love and belonging." She distinguishes shame from guilt, noting that while guilt is about feeling bad for something we've done ("I did something bad"), shame is about feeling bad about who we are ("I am bad"). Brown emphasizes that shame thrives in secrecy, silence, and judgment, and that speaking about our shame and owning our story are crucial steps in overcoming it.

Our complex relationship with money has exacerbated our relationship with shame. A budget only intensifies these feelings because it makes us feel like we lack willpower or have done something irresponsible. Building a healthy relationship with our finances is less about the money itself and more about understanding our emotions and patterns.

Our relationship with money is almost entirely emotional.

Meet Gail. Her husband's job required them to move to Las Vegas, tearing Gail away from the heart of her world—her family in the Midwest. The pain of leaving behind the close-knit connections she cherished was profound, making the transition even more difficult.

Gail did not want to move to Las Vegas. Gail was resentful. Because of that resentment and their resulting lack of communication, Gail started spending money however she wanted, and her husband didn't say anything about it. Her disconnect from their finances stemmed from an emotional disruption in her family.

Imagine waking up one day to discover that your household budget has hemorrhaged over $50,000 without your knowledge. This was Gail's reality—a crushing revelation that felt like a train wreck, leaving her reeling in disbelief and despair.

Gail's journey is not just a story of financial behavioral missteps. And, the further she and I dug into it, the budget was the mask that she and her husband were both holding onto that everything was "fine." Nothing was fine, and financially, there were secrets and misalignment. The weekly budgeting app was a facade. But as long as the numbers were reconciled at the end of the month, everything was "fine."

This is not just Gail and Swifty's story. This is the story of countless households on the planet.

Gail and Swifty's financial life turned around once they both took a long hard look in the mirror. Radical responsibility uncovering denial, resentment, and shame was the path to healing. Not budgeting. Initially, the weight of the financial secrets between Gail and her husband threatened to shatter their marriage. The betrayal stung, and the numbers were overwhelming. But instead of succumbing to the role of a victim, Gail chose a path of accountability.

With raw honesty, she and her husband began to peel back the layers of their financial downfall. They confronted painful truths, held each other accountable, and took deliberate, strategic actions to mend their fractured relationship. It wasn't just about crunching numbers—it was about healing a relationship strained by secrecy and resentment.

Gail's story shines a light on the profound connection between our internal world and our external realities. She realized that their financial chaos mirrored inner turmoil. By leaning into her authentic self, recognizing her brain-wired strengths, and embracing her unique superpowers, she began to navigate the tumultuous waters with renewed confidence.

Central to their recovery was the establishment of systems that simplified financial decisions. Open communication became their lifeline, supported by trustworthy friends, a nurturing community, and safe spaces where they could unravel and rebuild.

As Brené Brown would say, they spoke their truth out loud. They uncovered the real pain; they had the courage to see and be seen. That's when their healing began.

Through this journey, Gail understood that both budgets and relationships falter without honesty and mutual effort.

One of the most transformative shifts for Gail was redefining her relationship with time. She observed that how she allocated her hours directly influenced her bank statements. By making conscious lifestyle and behavioral changes, she set into motion a new sequence of events that propelled them toward financial stability.

Gail's poignant lesson resonates deeply: Our finances are a mirror, reflecting the intricate tapestries of our inner selves and our emotions. When we muster the courage to look beneath the surface, to confront our vulnerabilities, and to take purposeful action, we pave the way for profound change. Her story is a testament to the indomitable human spirit and the incredible transformations that await when we choose to face our challenges head-on.

> Fifty thousand dollars in credit card debt. They had a budget. How did this happen?

Spending money hadn't been about actual desires or needs, but a way to relieve stress and unconsciously retaliate.

The finance industry has long been propelled by a dynamic of shame, a powerful yet destructive force that subtly coerces many of us into silence and compliance. The narrative has been clear: If you're not wealthy, you're not trying hard enough, or you're spending foolishly. Such messages permeate our culture, making some pundits very wealthy by capitalizing on the insecurity and shame of others. This part of the conversation around money desperately needs to change.

Gail and her husband's journey through debt is a testament to why reverting to strict budgeting often fails to address the underlying emotional dynamics. Budgets can be useful tools, but when they become the sole focus, we miss the emotional and relational aspects of financial management. The cycle of shame that surrounds debt and financial struggle does nothing to foster real change or understanding; instead, it often deepens the problem, making it harder to see a way out.

To truly transform our relationship with money, especially as women who historically have been marginalized in financial conversations, we must shift the dialogue toward compassion, kindness, and curiosity. It's about understanding that feeling alive and truly living isn't captured in the numbers of a budget spreadsheet, but in the richness of our daily experiences—connecting, feeling, and sharing moments of joy and challenge alike.

Feeling alive—truly living—is about connection. It's emotional, honest, and raw. It's about listening actively, breathing deeply, touching, kissing, loving, hugging, giving, smiling, and embracing both sunrises and sunsets. It's about just being, existing in a moment without the shadow of financial shame darkening the experience.

For years, I ran from my problems as a way to feel alive, using spending as a justification for existence. This escape is a common story for many, where financial decisions are less about genuine need or desire and more about filling a void or proving worth. This approach is fundamentally flawed because it's built on a foundation of judgment and external validation, not self-acceptance and internal worth.

The remedy to financial shame is not more judgment or appointing self-proclaimed experts who dictate rigid paths to success. Instead, we need to foster environments where financial education is coupled with emotional intelligence, where questions are encouraged and mistakes are seen as opportunities for growth. By adopting a mindset of curiosity and kindness toward ourselves and our financial situations, we can begin to untangle the deep-seated beliefs that keep us trapped in cycles of shame and inadequacy.

This shift in conversation is essential for women to turn the corner in financial dialogues. We need to reclaim our power, not by adopting harsh self-discipline that echoes patriarchal values, but by understanding and nurturing our unique financial paths and respecting our diverse experiences and backgrounds.

Embracing this new approach means recognizing that our worth isn't tied to our bank accounts or financial acumen. It's about building a life where financial decisions support our values and visions, not one where they generate stress or diminish our sense of self. It's time to change the narrative around money, to strip away the shame and build a foundation of empowerment and genuine engagement with our finances. This is how we turn the corner: by insisting on a conversation that uplifts, educates, and embraces every woman's financial journey with open hearts and open minds.

JOURNALING PROMPTS

Stop Budgeting, Start Living
Heal the Shame

1. Reflect on Your Financial Shame

   What are some financial decisions or habits that have made you feel ashamed? How have these feelings of shame impacted your relationship with money?

2. Identify the Source of Judgment

   Think about a time when you felt judged by others (or yourself) for your financial choices. Where do you think this judgment originated from? How does it align or conflict with your personal values?

3. Exploring Emotional Spending

   Consider a time when you spent money as a way to cope with emotions like stress, resentment, or loneliness. What were you trying to achieve emotionally through that spending? How did it affect your financial well-being?

4. Unpacking Financial Secrecy

   Have you ever kept financial secrets from a partner, family member, or friend? What emotions were driving that secrecy? How might honesty have changed the situation?

5. Shifting the Narrative Around Money

   How would your life be different if you approached your financial decisions with compassion and curiosity instead of judgment and shame? What steps can you take to start making that shift?

6. Radical Responsibility and Healing

   Reflect on a time when taking radical responsibility for a financial mistake led to personal growth or healing. What did you learn about yourself through that process?

7. Redefining Your Relationship with Time and Money

   How do you currently spend your time, and how does that align with your financial goals? What changes can you make to better align your time with the financial life you want to create?

8. Building a Supportive Financial Community

   Who in your life can you turn to for open and honest conversations about money? How can you contribute to creating a supportive, nonjudgmental space for financial discussions?

9. Embracing Emotional Intelligence in Finances

   How can you incorporate more emotional intelligence into your financial decisions? What practices or habits can you adopt to better understand and manage the emotions tied to your money?

10. Transforming Financial Shame into Empowerment

What is one area of your financial life where you've felt shame but now see an opportunity for empowerment? How can you take the first step toward transforming that shame into a source of strength?

SET POINT

You have money now, but you weren't raised with it, and deep down, you feel a lingering sense of shame.

You're drowning in debt, yet you grew up surrounded by abundance, and somehow, you still feel ashamed.

Your mom used to hide shopping bags from your dad. Shame.

No two people share the same financial history, upbringing, or imprinting. Every single one of us carries a unique financial story written long before we had the language to understand it.

This is why it's profoundly important to understand where your financial shame, fear, anxiety, or overwhelm stems from.

You are the only one who can heal your financial life because you're the only one who has lived it.

Every person has a financial **set point**, an invisible line etched into the unconscious mind before the age of seven. This set point acts as a financial thermostat, quietly regulating your beliefs, habits, and actions around money. It determines how much you feel you're capable of earning, how much you allow yourself to save, and even how much you believe you're worth.

Your set point is shaped by what you saw, heard, and felt during your formative years. It's a byproduct of your environment, the behaviors of your caregivers, and societal messaging. If you grew up in a household where money was always tight, your set point likely reflects scarcity—always bracing for the next crisis. On the other hand, if you were surrounded by abundance, your set point may tie worth to success or performance, creating its own pressures.

This financial programming lives in the unconscious mind, and without awareness, it governs every financial decision you make.

BOB'S STORY

Let me introduce you to Bob. Bob wasn't just anyone—he was the former CEO of Tony Robbins' company, a multimillionaire who climbed to the pinnacle of professional success. Yet behind the polished exterior and accolades, Bob was a man at war with himself.

Bob's financial set point was forged in a childhood marked by poverty and economic insecurity. Growing up, his family scraped by, always worried about how to make ends meet. From an early age, Bob vowed he would never feel that kind of fear again. He believed wealth was the solution to every problem, the antidote to every worry.

And for a while, it seemed like he was right. Bob's career skyrocketed. He amassed wealth most people can only dream of, with a multimillion-dollar portfolio, eight Rolex watches, a wardrobe filled with custom-tailored suits, and a lifestyle that screamed success. But behind the scenes, Bob was unraveling.

His financial set point, rooted in the belief that "more is the answer," became his greatest downfall. No matter how much he earned, it was never enough. He turned to gambling to fill the void, placing bets that grew increasingly reckless. Addiction took hold—first to powdered cocaine, then to crack. The millions in his bank account weren't enough to save him from himself.

Bob's life spiraled out of control. He lost his career, his home, and the respect of those around him. Homeless and bankrupt, he hit rock bottom. But rock bottom wasn't the end of Bob's story—it was the beginning of his transformation.

In the depths of despair, Bob faced the truth he had been avoiding for years. His relentless chase for wealth wasn't about the money—it was about trying to fill the void of unworthiness and fear created in his childhood. This realization wasn't just painful; it was liberating.

"I had to lose everything to understand what truly mattered," Bob later reflected. *"The wealth I was chasing couldn't fix the emptiness I felt inside."*

Bob made the courageous decision to heal—not just from addiction, but from the wounds that shaped his financial set point. He immersed himself in therapy, reflecting on the patterns and beliefs that had driven him for decades. He rebuilt his life from the ground up, this time guided by purpose rather than fear.

Today, Bob channels his entrepreneurial spirit into meaningful pursuits that align with his values. He mentors others, sharing his story with vulnerability and honesty to help them break free from the traps he once fell into. His financial decisions are now rooted in peace and purpose, not the endless pursuit of "enough."

WHAT CAN YOU LEARN FROM BOB?

Bob's story is a powerful reminder that your financial set point is not your destiny. It may shape the way you approach money, but it doesn't have to define your future.

A budget cannot and will not fix what is broken within you.

Bob's transformation didn't come from spreadsheets or financial advisers—it came from confronting the beliefs that shaped his set point and doing the inner work to heal.

WHAT'S YOUR SET POINT?

Your financial set point may feel immovable, but here's the truth: It isn't set in stone. It can change, but only if you're willing to uncover its origins and intentionally reshape it.

Imagine your financial set point as a hiking trail you've walked every day of your life. It's familiar, even comforting, but it doesn't always lead where you want to go. Adjusting your set point requires stepping off the beaten path and forging a new one. It's uncomfortable at first, but with persistence, it becomes the path to the life you've always dreamed of.

Your financial set point matters. It shapes every aspect of your money life, from budgeting and investing to how you set—and achieve—your goals.

FINAL THOUGHT

"You can't fix what you don't face."

Acknowledging your set point is the first step. Embracing the challenge to heal it is the next. With awareness, effort, and the right tools, you can transform not only your financial habits but also your mindset.

Remember: Your financial set point is just a chapter in your story—not the whole book.

JOURNALING PROMPTS

Stop Budgeting, Start Living
Examining Your Own Financial Set Point

1. Identifying Your Financial Set Point

    Reflect on your upbringing and early experiences with money. What beliefs or attitudes about money were instilled in you before the age of seven? How has your set point influenced your financial decisions as an adult?

2. Exploring the Impact of Your Financial History

    How has your financial history, including any significant life events, shaped your current financial mindset? Are there patterns or behaviors that you recognize as being tied to past experiences?

3. Challenging Limiting Beliefs

    What are some limiting beliefs about money that you've identified in yourself? How have these beliefs held you back from achieving your financial goals? What steps can you take to challenge and change these beliefs?

4. Recognizing the Role of Emotions in Financial Decisions

    Consider a recent financial decision you made. What emotions were driving that decision? How might those emotions be connected to your financial set point?

5. Adjusting Your Financial Thermostat

   If you could change one financial habit or belief that no longer serves you, what would it be? What new belief or behavior would you like to adopt, and how can you start implementing it in your daily life?

6. Understanding External Influences

   How have societal messages about money, success, and worth impacted your financial set point? In what ways do these external influences align or conflict with your personal values?

7. Evaluating Financial Advice

   Think about financial advice you've received in the past. How did your financial set point influence your reception of that advice? How can you better discern advice that aligns with your personal financial philosophy?

8. Rewriting Your Financial Story

   If you were to write your financial story, what would the next chapter look like? What changes would you make to ensure your financial behaviors align with your aspirations and goals?

9. Creating a Supportive Financial Environment

   Who in your life understands and supports your financial journey? How will you build a community or find resources that align with your goals?

10. Taking Control of Your Financial Destiny

What is one actionable step you can take today to begin shifting your financial set point toward a more positive and inspiring direction? How will this step contribute to your overall financial well-being?

THE TOXICITY OF SHOULD

You don't need a Suze Orman or a Dave Ramsey or another financial expert making you feel bad about your decisions.

If you couldn't already tell, I'm not the biggest fan of my industry. There was a time very recently where I even considered leaving the industry all together. For a myriad of reasons, I was on the fence to leave. And, for the very reason I'm writing this book, I'm choosing to stay. For now.

> You don't need a Suze Orman or a Dave Ramsey or another financial expert making you feel bad about your decisions.

It's time for you to grab the reins and learn how you want to live your life, not according to how you should be living it.

I'm a rehab "should-er." I used to "should" myself all the time. I should do this, and I should do that. I'm a perfectionist in recovery, because I wanted my life to look perfect. It wasn't until I had the courage to release the shackles of what I thought my parents, my industry, my family, and my husband thought I should do that I began to live more freely. This has less to do with the amount of money in my bank account, although I do have systems and tools to stay on track financially.

Your own path is within you, and it's based on who you were born to be and how you were born to live. The dreams and desires in your heart need to be figured out first, and then we align your money in that direction. That's the work. A budget won't tell you what to do. A budget wants to engineer and control your money in a certain direction. It's never going to work. It hasn't until this point, so what do you have to lose by trying something new?

Our unconscious mind drives 95% of our brain activity, shaping how we think, feel, and make decisions—including what we buy. Harvard professor Gerald Zaltman highlights this in *How Customers Think*, showing that most of our purchasing decisions aren't rational—they're driven by emotions and subconscious patterns. When we understand this, we can stop operating on autopilot and start making choices that align with our values and goals. If we're not aware of our own beliefs and values about money, we face internal conflict. We say we want one thing but do the opposite, leading to self-conflict. My financial sabotage nearly led to rock bottom because I wasn't honest with myself and didn't know how to get unstuck. Coaches and NLP helped me tap into my unconscious mind, break through, and move forward.

For those feeling financially stuck, I'll offer some tips, but understand that budgeting alone won't fix the conflict between what you want and what you do. A budget is just a superficial fix without addressing the underlying mindset. Many people find traditional budgeting too analytical and restrictive. Instead, try a new approach to align your money with your true desires and values.

One way to begin to alleviate the shame is to recognize that you are not the same as others and that there is no one human on this planet who has the same approach to success as the other. The approach I'm offering in this book is not an easy way. It takes work, and if you're ready to get to work, I want to start with the first step you can take to stare shame in the face and tell it to fuck off.

Understanding your money personality is not just insightful; it's like discovering you're part of a financial Breakfast Club where everyone is convinced their way is the high road, especially the Saver, who often ends up like the class president—admirable, but a bit too buttoned-up for the rest of the gang. With the wisdom of Robyn Crane, let's dive into the five distinct money personalities, each bringing their own flair (and quirks) to the economic table:

1. *The Spender*: Think of the life of the party—present, fun, and always up for a spontaneous road trip. Spenders navigate life with a sense of abundance, turning every financial decision into a celebration. They're like that friend who insists on ordering dessert for the table… every time.
2. *The Saver*: Picture a person with a calculator for a brain, methodical and always ten steps ahead. Savers are the ones at the supermarket with a stack of coupons and a strategic plan to conquer the aisles. They're fantastic in a financial crisis but might just rain on your parade by reminding you about retirement savings at your birthday party.
3. *The Giver*: The warm heart, always ready with a hug or a helping hand. Givers are less interested in growing their wealth and more in growing their community.

They're like the generous grandma who always slips you a twenty, even when it's her own birthday.
4. *The Dreamer*: Big thinkers and risk-takers, Dreamers are the ones with their heads in the clouds and their ideas out of this world. They're the startup founders who pitch an app that sounds like sci-fi and then turn it into reality. They're inspiring but might forget to pay their electricity bill while chasing their next big breakthrough.
5. *The Avoider*: Ever the optimist, the Avoider has an aversion to conflict and a penchant for positivity that can turn any financial pit into a pinnacle. They're the delightful dinner guests who divert the conversation from politics to puppies. However, ask them about their credit score, and they might suddenly remember they left the oven on.

The beauty of understanding these personalities isn't just about navigating your financial landscape; it's about celebrating the diversity in our approaches. Yes, the Saver might secretly believe they wear the financial crown, and occasionally their thrifty-is-nifty attitude might alienate the more free-spirited Spender. But here's the twist: We all think everyone should be like us, and in doing so, we risk isolating ourselves.

By identifying which money personality resonates with you, you can begin to harness your natural strengths and approach your financial life with confidence and clarity. It's not about squeezing into a predefined box; it's about embracing how you naturally interact with money to create a more empowered and satisfying financial journey.

For instance, as a Giver who dreams big, I've had to learn that while my heart leads my wallet, I still need practical money management strategies. This meant delegating those tasks to someone whose heartbeat syncs with spreadsheets and analysis.

Understanding your money personality also paves the way for financial confidence. It allows you to align your spending with what truly matters to you. For example, realizing that my values lay more with family and joy than running a multimillion-dollar empire was a game changer. It helped me focus on what really enriches my life—beyond the balance sheet.

So, give yourself permission to spend *wisely and joyfully*. Move money into a spending account and relish in making choices that resonate with your life's values. Remember, women control a vast portion of consumer spending yet hold a sliver of the world's wealth. It's time to claim our financial power and spend with intention and insight.

Breaking free from traditional financial constraints begins with recognizing your money personality and aligning your spending to mirror your true values. This understanding marks the start of a renewed relationship with yourself, stepping out of the "should" box into a life of financial freedom and fulfillment. And now, the next question: What is stopping you from doing something you know you want to do?

Curious about which money personality best describes you? Take the quiz!

lisachastain.com/quiz

JOURNALING PROMPTS

Stop Budgeting, Start Living
Stop Shoulding All Over Yourself

1. Reflecting on the "Shoulds" in Your Life

    What are some "shoulds" that you have internalized when it comes to your financial decisions? How have these "shoulds" influenced your actions and feelings about money?

2. Identifying Your Money Personality

    After learning about the different money personalities, which one are you? How has this personality influenced your financial behaviors, both positively and negatively?

3. Breaking Free from External Expectations

    Think about a financial decision you made based on what you felt you "should" do rather than what you truly wanted. How did that decision impact your sense of fulfillment and well-being? What would you do differently now?

4. Aligning Your Money with Your Values

    What are your core values, and how do they align (or conflict) with your current financial habits? What steps can you take to ensure that your financial decisions better reflect what truly matters to you?

5. Reclaiming Financial Power

   In what ways can you take back control of your financial life by rejecting the "shoulds" imposed by society, experts, or even yourself? What specific actions can you take to start living according to your own financial guidelines?

6. Embracing Your Financial Strengths

   What are the natural strengths of your money personality? How can you use these strengths to create a more empowered and satisfying financial journey?

7. Exploring Financial Sabotage

   Have you ever sabotaged your financial success due to internal conflict between what you want and what you think you "should" do? How can you begin to resolve this conflict and move forward?

8. Setting Personal Financial Goals

   What are some financial goals that truly excite and inspire you, regardless of what others might think or say? How can you start taking steps toward achieving these goals in a way that feels authentic to you?

9. Taking Action Toward Financial Freedom

   What is one financial "should" you are ready to let go of today? How will releasing this "should" help you move closer to a life of financial freedom and fulfillment?

STARING FEAR IN THE FACE

Nothing makes us feel more vulnerable than money fears. In my financial free fall, I was scared to ask for help because I felt others would judge me. Fear of being judged is such a huge common obstacle that a lot of people have, and I am definitely no exception.

I was a financial adviser; how could I not know how to manage my own money?!

I knew I was lacking, but what I didn't realize at the time was that I was not alone.

> **I was a financial adviser; how could I not know how to manage my own money?!**

Things like worrying about making a mistake, making a wrong money move, and then being open to judgment from people like significant others, parents, peers, the neighbor, and others is more common than you may realize. Over sixty million Americans are carrying debt, a burden that impacts so much more than just their bank accounts.

In 2024, the average debt rose from $21,800 to $22,713, with 66 percent of people admitting they have at least some debt. Credit cards account for 28 percent of this, while auto loans make up another 13 percent, numbers that haven't changed much since 2023, according to Northwestern Mutual.

As it turns out, a lot of people are in the very same situation, yet you'd never know it because debt has become such a shameful topic. This silence keeps people stuck, but it doesn't have to be that way.

Being vulnerable with our money means putting down the judgment fears so you don't have to keep up with anyone and, most importantly, with yourself.

Maybe you're stuck in a job you despise, waking up every day with a sense of dread that weighs heavy on your chest. The hours drag on, and no matter how hard you try to push through, the dissatisfaction gnaws at you, leaving you feeling trapped and exhausted. Then there's the rent—it's due in just a few days, and you're coming up short. The anxiety builds as you wonder how you'll make ends meet this month. Debt collectors are relentless, their calls a constant reminder of the financial hole that feels impossible to climb out of. The stress is suffocating, and you're overwhelmed by a sense of failure and hopelessness.

But even if your bank account had plenty of money, the fear of facing your finances might still paralyze you. The thought of logging into your accounts, of seeing the reality of your situation in black and white, is terrifying. What if it's worse than you thought? What if it reveals mistakes you didn't realize you made, or confirms that sinking feeling that you're not in control?

So you avoid it, convincing yourself that ignoring the problem will somehow make it go away. But deep down, you know that avoidance only compounds the anxiety. The fear of the unknown, of what you might uncover, keeps you stuck in a cycle of stress and avoidance. Money, whether abundant or scarce, becomes a source of dread rather than a tool for security and peace of mind.

This avoidance isn't just about the numbers—it's about what those numbers represent. They're tied to your sense of self-worth, your ability to provide, your dreams and fears. Facing your finances means confronting the parts of your life that feel out of control, the vulnerabilities you'd rather not acknowledge.

It's about more than just dollars and cents; it's about confronting the emotional weight that money carries and the stories you tell yourself about what it means for your life.

> **It's about more than just dollars and cents; it's about confronting the emotional weight that money carries and the stories you tell yourself about what it means for your life.**

The idea of trying something new and failing isn't fun. It's so scary that people will actively avoid trying anything new just so they don't have to fail at it. Some fear comes from past failures, some comes from imagined failures. But the thing about failure is that it means you're trying. It means you are learning. Failure means you are getting that much closer to success.

Our experiences shape our reactions, our attitudes, and our general approaches toward life. Challenges—whether expected or unexpected—can start to feel like failure. The steps to elevating our finances aren't always graceful! Sometimes you will stumble, and sometimes you might even fall, but it's important to keep moving forward.

Fear limits our movements, it limits our willingness to put ourselves out there, and it limits our opportunities to succeed. Ironic, isn't it? The very thing that we use to protect ourselves from rejection and failure can keep us from not being successful in the long run.

The distant relative of the fear of failure is the fear of success—and it's far more common than you might think. Does this sound familiar? Fear of success is often rooted in unconscious feelings of inadequacy, feeling unworthy or unable to either reach or maintain the goal. Add in a dollop of impostor syndrome and you've got yourself a recipe for being afraid to succeed. What if you fail? What if the dream is not what you expected? What if you end up disillusioned? What if you got duped? The list can go on and on. It's the fear of false success, the fear of somehow feeling not worthy of the positive outcome that holds you back. Understanding that the fear of success exists will help you recognize it when it happens to you.

I had a deep-seated fear—a belief that if I became incredibly successful and my business took off, my husband would not support me. I feared that my career ambitions would distance me from my family and leave me without the support I needed. This fear, that if my desires and dreams became too big, I would lose the support of my husband, still haunts me to this day. I know I'm not alone in this fear. Recently, I was in a room with twenty women who echoed the same concern. As women in business, we must confront these fears, get curious about them, and lean into them. The future of the world depends on us, and it will be women like us who pave the way to a healthier, more equitable world. We cannot let our fears hold us back.

Where did my fear come from? My father. There's a lot to unpack here. As a forty-four-year-old woman, I realize that it wasn't really my father holding me back—it was my own fear. But, before the inner work I did, as a young woman, I believed that if I dreamed "too big" and played "too big," I wouldn't be supported. Where'd that come from? My father telling me not to dream big, go big, or risk big. Consequently, I feared rejection and shame if I stepped too far outside the box. This fear wasn't unfounded; there were times when my family didn't support me in the choices I was making. But it was in these very moments that I learned the most. By feeling the fear and rejection, I was faced with a choice: to lean into it and walk through the fire, or to let it consume me.

Time and again, I chose to walk through the fire—the pain, the shame, the fear. As a result of standing up for my desires and purpose, I have had to let go of relationships, including my first marriage. I allowed fear to keep me safe and small for fifteen years, until I simply couldn't take it anymore.

Money fears can also come from more complicated life experiences, especially relationships. Whether you're married, in a partner relationship, or any other kind of arrangement where you're financially even slightly connected to someone special, fear can start to take bigger and stranger shapes. Thoughts like: Can you still be free to make your own money decisions? Do you feel safe and stable, money-wise, with respect to your partner. Do you trust your partner's attitudes and actions toward finances? Our partners affect our money, and their habits impact ours, even if we're not sharing a bank account. The biggest money mistake that couples make with money? Not talking about it!

Money is a major stressor for relationships. It can lead to divorce, keep you trapped in a toxic relationship, and do anything in between. Fear can make it difficult to have tough conversations; it's scary to show our bank accounts or our credit card statements if we've been hiding those numbers. I've been there. And it left me stuck in a toxic relationship until I had the courage to step away and work toward my own financial stability.

Fear of making a mistake is another big one. Some of us can relate to the hesitation and lack of confidence that can come from feeling too intimidated to make a move. Money is such a huge and complicated thing in life, and one that most of us were never taught in grade school. It can leave you paralyzed if you don't know what to do first. If you screw something up, what happens next? That's the fear from unfamiliarity, and the power of self-preservation kicking in. What if a big mistake costs you money and then sets you way back, or brings about a bunch of criticism or judgment from other people? Fear can make you so afraid to take action on anything, but then you'll get nothing done.

I was in a sixteen-year marriage, and for a long time, I blamed him for everything. It wasn't my fault; it was his. But here's the truth, and I say this with a background in neuroscience. It would be easy to blame someone else, but actually, there's this box of shame that's been created. In the finance industry, for many reasons, things aren't working. How do I know this? Because I keep having the same conversations with clients, online, on podcasts, on stages, in groups, and in masterminds. People are tired. They're tired of being beaten down and beaten up. There has to be another way. They've tried budgets, but they don't work. They've tried other methods, but they don't work either.

There is another way, but we need to confront the conversations we've had about personal finance for years. For years, we've been told, yelled at, screamed at, and made to feel like idiots for making bad choices. We've been told to change our behaviors, and that if we have credit card debt, we should feel ashamed. Because of these conversations, I was in my shame box for so long. Financially, I was trapped. My life didn't look perfect; it was falling apart. I needed help and a place for real, open, honest conversations.

At the same time, we're being berated by the media, commercials, Instagram, apps, and ads telling us we need certain things to be happy. We've been fed this stuff since we could watch TV. It's not all your fault. I'm saying this with compassion, love, and understanding of how our brains work.

Today, let this be your interruption to realize *it's not your fault*.

And now, it is your responsibility, and you can reset your financial life.

So, for just a minute, can we take a breath?

Can we just decide to do something different? We're going to stop beating our heads against the wall. We're going to stop doing things that haven't worked for years.

We're going to forgive ourselves and take new steps in a new direction so we can finally figure out what we want and how our money can help us get there.

It's about getting our lives together first, and then our money will follow. Have you seen the movie *The Pursuit of Happyness*? It's one of my favorites. We just rewatched it with our kids.

The movie has a lot of life lessons. There's a character, Christopher, who is hustling to sell medical imaging devices in San Francisco, trying to make it big while supporting his son; he's a *big* Dreamer. Christopher's wife, who values security, gets frustrated because there's no steady paycheck, leading to constant arguments about money. She's a big-time Saver. This mirrors many of our lives. If it's not our significant other we're battling with, it's ourselves.

Our relationships with money are the sources of every positive and negative outcome in our financial lives. It's the number-one source of conflict in relationships. Your relationship with money impacts all areas of your life.

To transform and reset your relationship with money this year, you have to start with yourself.

Remember, it starts young. Our relationship with money starts at a very young age, during the imprinting years. Neuroscientists and psychologists agree that before age seven, we form beliefs and decisions about ourselves and money. If you never address what happened in your life before age seven, a seven-year-old is essentially running your financial life. And let's be honest, seven-year-olds don't know much about money or themselves.

Today is the best day and opportunity to question what influenced your financial set point.

> **Today is the best day and opportunity to question what influenced your financial set point.**

For me, there was always a conversation about not having enough. I was a surprise to my parents, and they constantly worried about money. This influenced my relationship with money until I had the courage to confront my mindset. I attracted some really toxic relationships because of my unworthy conversation. And as I write this to you, I'm fighting a mild shame that is telling me that I "should" not be sharing with you that I'm not perfect. Somehow, I believe you're also relieved to know that I'm not perfect.

Today, I have a healthy relationship with money, even though I'm not debt free. And that's okay. Debt is not the nemesis of my life, but it used to be. Why?

Listening to Dave Ramsey and similar pundits, how could it not be?

The most important work is to understand your relationship with money and address any limiting beliefs.

My financial sabotage nearly led to rock bottom because I wasn't being honest with myself. And, truthfully, I had no idea what was in my way. I had so many blind spots (we all do).

Good coaches help you tap into your unconscious mind and get unstuck. This isn't something you can do on your own, even with books and journal exercises. Coaches help you break through and move forward.

If you're feeling stuck financially, you must take a deeper dive into your relationship with money to align your money with your true desires and values. Traditional budgeting is too analytical and restrictive for many people. Instead, break up with your budget and commit to trying something new. If what you've been doing hasn't worked, let's reset your system and try a new approach.

The shame machine keeps us on a financial roller coaster. How many of you have been on this roller coaster for too long? You feel great when you have money, but when you don't, you feel shame and fear. This cycle has to stop. Your budget won't fix it, so throw it out. It's time to carve a new path and think for yourself financially. You don't need another financial expert telling you what to do. It's time for you to grab the reins and live your life according to your own values and dreams.

For those feeling financially stuck, I'll offer some tips, but understand that budgeting alone won't fix the conflict between what you want and what you do. A budget is just a superficial fix without addressing the underlying mindset. Many people find traditional budgeting too analytical and restrictive. Instead, try a new approach to align your money with your true desires and values.

JOURNALING PROMPTS

Stop Budgeting, Start Living
Feel Fear, Take Action Anyway

1. Identifying Your Money Fears

   What are some of the biggest fears you have when it comes to money? How do these fears influence your financial decisions and your overall sense of security?

2. Reflecting on Fear of Judgment

   Think about a time when you avoided addressing a financial issue because you feared being judged by others. How did this fear affect your actions, and what was the outcome?

3. Confronting the Fear of Failure

   In what ways has the fear of making a financial mistake held you back? What steps can you take to face this fear and make decisions with greater confidence?

4. Exploring Fear of Success

   Have you ever felt afraid of what might happen if you achieved financial success? What underlying beliefs or insecurities are tied to this fear, and how can you begin to address them?

5. Understanding the Impact of Early Influences

   Reflect on your childhood and early experiences with money. How did these experiences shape your current fears and beliefs about money? What lessons or messages from your past are still influencing you today?

6. Breaking the Cycle of Avoidance

   Is there a financial issue or task you've been avoiding out of fear? What might happen if you faced it head-on? Write about the potential benefits of confronting this issue and how you can take the first step.

7. Building Financial Resilience

   What practices or habits can you adopt to strengthen your resilience in the face of financial challenges? How can you use your past experiences to inform and empower your future decisions?

8. Releasing Shame Around Money

   How has shame around money shown up in your life? What would it look like to let go of this shame and approach your financial situation with compassion and understanding?

9. Creating a New Money Narrative

   If you could rewrite your story about money, fear, and success, what would it look like? How would your new narrative empower you to make more confident and aligned financial choices?

10. Taking Responsibility for Your Financial Future

What does taking responsibility for your financial life mean to you? How can you start taking proactive steps today to move past fear and toward the financial life you truly desire?

PART TWO
OWNERSHIP

• • • •

You are imperfect, permanently and inevitably flawed…And you are beautiful.
—*Amy Bloom*

FREEDOM IS ON THE OTHER SIDE OF PERFECTIONISM

As women, we're constantly bombarded with the unrealistic expectation of perfection across every aspect of our lives, be it as mothers, professionals, partners, or friends. As a frequent in the media I'm regularly subjected to harsh criticism of others. The worst part of all of the feedback has been the feedback I give to myself.

In my pursuit of perfection, I was the one hurting myself the most. My freedom has been earned from telling my perfectionism to take a hike.

America Ferrera's *Barbie* monologue struck a chord with so many women:

> It is literally impossible to be a woman. You are so beautiful and so smart, and it kills me that you don't think you're good enough. We have to always be extraordinary, but somehow

we're always doing it wrong. You have to be thin, but not too thin, and you can never say you want to be thin. You have to say you want to be healthy, but also you have to be thin. You have to have money, but you can't ask for money because that's crass. You have to be a boss, but you can't be mean. You have to lead, but you can't squash other people's ideas. You're supposed to love being a mother, but don't talk about your kids all the time. You have to be a career woman, but also always be looking out for other people. You have to answer for men's bad behavior, which is insane. But if you point that out, you're accused of complaining. You're supposed to stay pretty for men, but not so pretty that you tempt them too much or that you threaten other women because you're supposed to be part of the sisterhood, but always stand out and always be grateful. But never forget that the system is rigged. So find a way to acknowledge that, but also always be grateful. You have to never get old, never be rude, never show off, never be selfish, never fall down, never fail, never show fear, never get out of line. It's too hard, it's too contradictory, and nobody gives you a medal or says thank you. And it turns out, in fact, that not only are you doing everything wrong, but also everything is your fault. I'm just so tired of watching myself and every single other woman tie herself into knots so that people will like us. And if all of that is also true for a doll just representing a woman, then I don't even know.

What would happen if we stopped chasing this illusion and instead, embraced living beautifully imperfect lives?

What freedoms might that unlock for you?

The push for perfection isn't just a personal battle; it's an ideology perpetuated by industries like coaching and social media. These platforms often create a culture of dependency, subtly—or not so subtly—suggesting that we need these people's guidance to succeed. This idea that solutions lie outside ourselves not only undermines our autonomy but also feeds into destructive beliefs like "I'm not smart enough" or "I'm not worthy."

These are the shackles that prevent us from making autonomous decisions, particularly in our financial lives, driving us toward frustration and self-doubt.

Let's set the record straight: No expert holds all the answers for your life. Effective coaches don't spoon-feed solutions; they facilitate the process of discovery, helping you to unearth the insights that resonate deeply within you. *You are the ultimate authority on your life.* It's time to dismantle the notions of perfection and external validation.

Imagine the possibilities if we released the grip of perfection. What if we allowed ourselves the space to make mistakes, to learn from them, and to evolve? Trusting our intuition and inner wisdom could transform our lives into rich tapestries of authenticity and fulfillment, free from the fear of judgment.

Living imperfectly means accepting the messiness of life—the highs and lows, the victories and challenges—with grace and resilience. Our value isn't measured by our flawlessness but by how we present ourselves, connect with others, and care for ourselves.

Often, the fear of imperfection stems from a deep-seated desire for control, especially prevalent among women who have experienced tumultuous upbringings where control equated to survival. For me, this need transformed into an unhealthy obsession with perfection, which eventually led to a profound personal breakdown.

Control is not merely about managing outcomes; it's a survival tactic. When things feel out of control, it's not just uncomfortable—it feels downright life-threatening. In my darkest moments, I believed that losing control meant facing death. This overwhelming fear pushed me to extremes to avoid vulnerability at all costs.

But here's the kicker—this fear is a monstrous lie, a story we tell ourselves that keeps us trapped in a vicious cycle of avoidance and hypercontrol. Working with my NLP coach, Stacey, was transformative. She illuminated that my avoidance was not a flaw but a deeply ingrained survival mechanism. It wasn't until I confronted this fear head-on that I began to dismantle the narratives that held me captive.

Letting go of the illusion of control is not optional; it's essential for reclaiming the life that fear has stolen from us. While we can't control everything, we can choose how we respond to life's uncertainties. We can choose to engage deeply, to be present, and to embrace life's unpredictability.

The narrative propagated by the coaching industry and social media—that we need them to succeed—is fundamentally flawed. It fosters a dependency that keeps us returning for more, perpetuating the cycle of self-doubt, particularly around financial decisions.

It's time to challenge the narrative that demands perfection and external guidance. What if we embraced our imperfections?

What if we trusted ourselves to navigate our mistakes and learn from them? Our lives would be authentically rich, unshackled by the fear of inadequacy, allowing us to live freely and boldly.

What do we truly desire? Through my experiences and interactions with thousands of women, I've learned that we crave deep connections, joyous engagements, and a profound sense of being alive. We long for laughter that echoes from our souls, for kisses that linger, and for embraces that complete us. We seek genuine interactions, the excitement of growth, and the serenity of just being.

We dream of a world where compassion reigns, where love transcends conflict, and where our children know without a doubt that they are enough. We envision a world where empathy is the norm, not the exception—a world where we rise together, united in our diversity.

Is this merely a dream, or is it a reality within our grasp? The truth is, nothing changes unless we do. It's our responsibility to initiate the healing, to live authentically, and by doing so, inspire others to follow suit.

You possess the power to forge the life you envision and to inspire others to embark on this journey with you. Start now, and witness the transformation not just in yourself, but in the world around you. Here and now, embrace the truth that you are enough just as you are. Your worth isn't tied to an unattainable standard of perfection.

The real strength lies not in clinging to control but in letting go and allowing life to unfold in all its messy, unpredictable beauty. This is where true growth occurs. This is where you find the courage to live a life that's richer, more meaningful, and authentically yours. Stop bullshitting yourself—it's time to take action.

JOURNALING PROMPTS

Stop Budgeting, Start Living
Reframing Perfectionism

1. Reflecting on Perfectionism

    How has the pursuit of perfection shown up in your life? In what areas do you feel the pressure to be perfect, and how has it impacted your well-being?

2. Recognizing Self-Criticism

    What are some of the harshest criticisms you direct at yourself? How do these criticisms affect your self-worth and your ability to live authentically?

3. Exploring the Desire for Control

    In what ways do you try to control outcomes in your life? How does this need for control relate to your fears and past experiences? What would happen if you let go of some of that control?

4. Embracing Imperfection

    Think about a time when you allowed yourself to be imperfect. How did that feel, and what did you learn from the experience? How can you bring more of this mindset into your daily life?

5. Challenging External Expectations

   What external expectations have you internalized about how you should live your life? How can you begin to dismantle these expectations and replace them with your own values and desires?

6. Trusting Your Inner Wisdom

   How often do you trust your intuition when making decisions? What might change in your life if you leaned more into your inner wisdom rather than seeking external validation?

7. Letting Go of Perfectionism

   What is one area of your life where you can start letting go of perfectionism? What steps can you take to embrace imperfection and allow yourself to grow and evolve naturally?

8. Claiming Your Autonomy

   How can you take back control of your life from the narratives that tell you you're not enough unless you're perfect? What actions can you take to assert your autonomy and live according to your true self?

9. Living Authentically

   What does living authentically mean to you? How can you begin to align your actions, decisions, and relationships with your true self, free from the fear of judgment?

10. Finding Freedom in Imperfection

What freedoms might you gain by releasing the need to be perfect? How would embracing your flaws and imperfections change the way you approach life, relationships, and your goals?

RADICAL RESPONSIBILITY

Radical responsibility changes the game, especially when it comes to tackling the challenges we're facing in our own lives. Once we get that part right, we can start addressing the bigger issues in the world—like environmental crises, social injustice, political instability, and economic inequality. It's easy to feel overwhelmed, powerless, and tempted to look to others for answers. But when we keep searching externally, we often miss our own power to create change. The world needs us to step up, to be the difference, and that starts with taking radical responsibility for our own lives.

OWN YOUR ROLE IN SHAPING YOUR LIFE

Radical responsibility is about acknowledging and embracing your role in shaping your life and, by extension, the world around you. It's the realization that while we may not control every event or circumstance, we always have the power to choose our response. This mindset shift from victimhood to responsibility is key to unlocking your personal freedom and potential.

It's about understanding that every choice, no matter how small, contributes to the larger picture of your life and the collective reality we all share.

Today, where we're constantly bombarded by noise—social media, news, societal pressures—it's becoming harder and harder to hear our own inner voice. The real issue here is that we've stopped trusting ourselves. We second-guess our instincts, doubting whether we really know what's best for us. Here's the paradox: The only way for us to make any changes that will make the difference is by tuning into our inner wisdom. It's your most reliable guide in a world full of conflicting opinions and advice. When you trust your intuition, you start making decisions that truly align with who you are, leading to a more fulfilling and authentic life.

SILENCE THE NOISE

We live in an age where external influences are louder than ever. Whether it's the latest trend, political rhetoric, or someone else's idea of success, the noise can drown out our own beliefs and desires. But it's not just the external noise that's the problem—many of us carry internal noise too. If you grew up in a household that was overly critical, with a narcissistic parent or around abuse, second-guessing yourself might have become a way of life. That internalized doubt can be even more damaging than anything from the outside. To take radical responsibility, we have to learn to silence both the external and internal noise. This doesn't mean disconnecting entirely from the world, but rather developing the discernment to filter out what doesn't serve us so we can start trusting ourselves again.

When we quiet the external noise, we can finally begin to hear what truly matters: our inner guidance. This internal compass is unique to each of us, shaped by our experiences, values, and aspirations. Trusting it is crucial not only for personal growth, but also for making meaningful contributions to the world. This is especially true in personal finance, where clarity is power. By silencing the pundits and experts, and by understanding who we truly are and what we genuinely want, we can live lives free from the toxic and unnecessary advice plaguing the industry right now. When we align our financial decisions with our true selves, we take control of our finances and create a ripple effect that positively impacts those around us and, by extension, the world.

GETTING OUT TO GAIN PERSPECTIVE

One of the most powerful ways I've found to silence the noise and get real with myself is through the retreats I lead every year, especially the ones to Zion. These retreats aren't just about having fun, drinking wine, and disconnecting from the daily grind. They're about something much deeper. They're about giving ourselves the space to get present, to listen to our inner voices, and to trust ourselves in ways we might not be able to in our everyday lives.

Every year, I take a group of women to a quiet destination, and we immerse ourselves in nature, far away from the distractions of our regular lives. It's a time to pause, reflect, and gain perspective on where we are and where we want to go. These retreats are transformative—not just for the women who attend, but for me as well. It's in these quiet moments, surrounded by the beauty and stillness of nature, that I've made some of the most important decisions about my life.

I've seen it happen time and again—women who arrive feeling overwhelmed and disconnected leave with a renewed sense of purpose and clarity. They realize that they have so much more to give to this world than they ever imagined. This is the power of silencing the noise around us. It's not just about getting away; it's about getting in touch with the deepest parts of ourselves.

IT'S BIGGER THAN YOU

The challenges facing the world today are immense, and they can make individual efforts feel insignificant. However, the collective power of individuals taking radical responsibility is profound. Imagine a world where everyone took ownership of their actions, where each person recognized their power to make a difference. This collective shift in mindset could lead to monumental changes on a global scale.

For example, consider the environmental crisis. It's easy to feel that our individual actions—recycling, reducing waste, conserving energy—are drops in the ocean compared to the scale of the problem. But when millions of people commit to these actions, the cumulative effect is significant. Moreover, taking radical responsibility in this context extends beyond our immediate actions. It involves advocating for change, supporting policies that protect the environment, and educating others about sustainable practices.

Similarly, in the realm of social justice, taking radical responsibility means examining our biases, challenging systemic inequalities, and using our voices to advocate for those who are marginalized. It's about recognizing that while we may not be able to solve these issues alone, our actions can contribute to a larger movement for change.

Radical responsibility is transformative, especially in our relationship with money and personal growth. Money is a major source of stress and anxiety, and too many of us are stuck in unhealthy financial habits. Taking radical responsibility means facing these habits head-on, understanding the beliefs behind them, and making conscious decisions to change.

Our relationship with money doesn't just shape our personal finances—it shapes our entire economy. And our economy is more than just numbers; it's our business, our way of life. There are some deeply toxic aspects of our economy—from the sex trade to child trafficking—that could be eradicated entirely if we had the courage to connect our purpose with money to something much greater than just acquiring a Louis Vuitton bag. Imagine if we shifted our focus from material possessions to using money as a tool for positive impact. By aligning our financial decisions with a higher purpose, we can play a part in dismantling these destructive systems and create an economy that reflects our true values and the kind of world we want to live in.

This process is not easy. It requires honesty, self-reflection, and a willingness to make difficult choices. But it's also incredibly empowering. When you take control of your finances, you reclaim your power. You stop letting money control your life and start using it as a tool to achieve your goals and dreams.

Personal growth, too, flourishes under the mantle of radical responsibility. Growth requires us to step out of our comfort zones, face our fears, and challenge our limitations. It demands that we stop blaming others for our circumstances and start taking action to change them. This kind of growth is not just about achieving success, but about becoming the best version of ourselves.

ROCK BOTTOM

Sadly, embracing radical responsibility often comes from hitting rock bottom. I've been there—in that dark, terrifying place where it feels like everything is crumbling. During my divorce, I found myself in a toxic rebound relationship that drained me emotionally and financially. I was staring down the very real possibility of homelessness, with my life in complete disarray. It was a moment of absolute desperation, the kind where you have no choice but to look in the mirror and confront the person staring back.

I was broken, shattered by the realization that it wasn't just circumstances or other people that had led me to this point—it was me. I had made choices, I had ignored red flags, and I had allowed myself to get to a place where everything felt like it was falling apart. It was in that moment of raw, painful clarity that I realized I couldn't blame anyone else for the mess I was in. I had created it, and if I wanted to change my life, I had to start by taking full responsibility for it.

There was no more running from the truth, no more hiding behind excuses. I had to own every part of my story—the good, the bad, and the downright ugly. It was a sobering and humbling experience, but it was also the first step toward reclaiming my life. By taking radical responsibility, I began to rebuild, piece by piece, learning to trust myself again and make decisions that aligned with the person I truly wanted to be. That moment, as painful as it was, became the foundation for a new life, one built on honesty, accountability, and the deep understanding that I am the author of my own story.

This is not an uncommon story. Many people experience a moment of reckoning when they realize that their lives are not what they want them to be. It's a painful but necessary step toward transformation.

When you take radical responsibility, you stop waiting for someone else to save you. You stop blaming others for your problems. Instead, you take ownership of your life and start making changes.

> **When you take radical responsibility, you stop waiting for someone else to save you.**

This process is not about self-blame or guilt; it's about personal power and authority. It's about recognizing that you have the power to change your life, no matter how dire your circumstances may seem. By embracing radical responsibility, you shift from being a passive observer of your life to being an active participant in creating your future.

BE THE DIFFERENCE

The world needs more people who are willing to take radical responsibility, not just for their own lives but for the future of humanity. We are at a critical juncture in history where our collective actions will determine the fates of our planet and our societies. *Each of us has a role to play in this.*

By stepping up, taking charge, and living with purpose, we can be the difference the world so desperately needs. This doesn't mean we have to solve all the world's problems ourselves. But by taking responsibility for our actions, making conscious choices, and living in alignment with our values, we contribute to the collective effort for positive change.

Radical responsibility is not just a personal philosophy; it's a way of life that has the power to transform individuals and, by extension, the world. In a world overwhelmed by noise and external influences, it calls us to listen to our inner wisdom, trust our intuitions, and take charge of our lives.

When we embrace radical responsibility, we acknowledge our power to shape our destiny and influence the world around us. This shift in mindset is life-changing. It empowers us to move from a place of fear and helplessness to one of strength and purpose. It challenges us to stop looking elsewhere for solutions and start creating the change we want to see.

The world needs us to step up, to be the difference.

The world needs us to take radical responsibility not just for our own lives, but for the futures of our planet and our societies. This goes beyond just managing our personal lives—it's about stepping up in every area that touches our world.

Our societies are a reflection of our collective actions and values. When we take radical responsibility, we contribute to building a society that values equity, justice, and sustainability. Imagine if each of us made conscious decisions that prioritize the well-being of others over personal gain. We could transform our communities into places where everyone has the opportunity to thrive.

Our education system is shaping the next generation of leaders, thinkers, and citizens. Schools need us to take responsibility by advocating for an education system that doesn't just teach to the test but nurtures critical thinking, creativity, and empathy. When we take radical responsibility for the kind of education our children receive, we help create a future where young people are equipped not just with knowledge, but with the wisdom to use it for good.

Faith communities have always been a place for moral and ethical guidance. But they too need us to take radical responsibility by ensuring that these institutions live up to the principles they preach. It's about pushing for inclusivity, compassion, and action that extends beyond the walls of the church to impact the broader community. When we hold our faith communities accountable, we strengthen their ability to be forces for good in the world.

The foundation of any society is the family. Our families need us to model radical responsibility by creating environments where love, respect, and accountability are the norms. When we take responsibility for our actions within our families, we teach our children the values that will guide them throughout their lives. We set the example for how to live with integrity, compassion, and purpose.

Our local communities are where we can see the immediate impact of taking radical responsibility. Whether it's through volunteering, supporting local businesses, or simply being a good neighbor, we help our communities thrive when we each do our part. When we take ownership of our roles within our communities, we build stronger, more resilient networks of support and cooperation.

The future belongs to our children, and they need us to take radical responsibility now. They're watching and learning from us every day. By demonstrating what it means to live with purpose, to care for others, and to stand up for what's right, we empower them to grow into adults who will continue to carry the torch of responsibility and change. Our kids need us to show them that they have the power to make a difference, starting with their own lives.

Our treatment of animals is a reflection of our values as a society. Animals need us to take radical responsibility by advocating for their protection and well-being. Whether it's through supporting humane practices, adopting pets, or protecting wildlife, our actions can make a significant impact. By taking responsibility for how we interact with and care for animals, we create a world that values all living beings.

Our planet is facing unprecedented challenges—climate change, loss of biodiversity, pollution, and more. The world needs us to take radical responsibility not just for our own lives, but for the future of our planet. This means making sustainable choices, advocating for policies that protect the environment, and educating others about the importance of preserving our natural world. The Earth is our shared home, and it needs each of us to step up and take action to protect it for future generations.

The call to take radical responsibility extends to every corner of our lives. Our societies, schools, churches, families, communities, kids, animals, and the planet itself are all counting on us. The world needs us to step up, to be the difference, and to create a future where all can thrive. It starts with us, and it starts now.

This is the call to action. It's time to silence the noise, take charge, and create the world we want to live in. The journey starts with each of us, and it must start today.

JOURNALING PROMPTS

Stop Budgeting, Start Living
First Steps to Responsibility

1. Reflecting on Personal Responsibility

   In what areas of your life do you feel you've been avoiding responsibility? How can you begin to take radical responsibility for these aspects and create positive change?

2. Acknowledging Your Power to Choose

   Think about a recent situation where you felt powerless or stuck. How might your response have been different if you had embraced your power to choose your reaction? What can you learn from this experience?

3. Silencing the Noise

   What external and internal "noise" do you struggle with the most? How can you begin to filter out these distractions and tune into your inner wisdom more effectively?

4. Understanding Your Role in Larger Issues

   Consider a global or societal issue that you care about deeply. What actions can you take, however small, to contribute to positive change in this area? How does taking responsibility in this way empower you?

5. Gaining Perspective Through Reflection

   Reflect on a time when you took a step back from your daily life (e.g., through a retreat, vacation, or quiet reflection). How did this experience help you gain clarity or perspective? How can you incorporate more of these moments into your life?

6. Connecting Personal Responsibility with Global Impact

   How do your personal choices and behaviors impact the world around you? In what ways can you align your daily actions with the broader changes you want to see in society?

7. Rebuilding After Rock Bottom

   Think about a time when you felt like you hit rock bottom. What steps did you take to rebuild your life? How did taking radical responsibility play a role in your recovery and growth?

8. Exploring the Impact of Radical Responsibility in Relationships

   How has taking responsibility for your actions and decisions improved your relationships with others? What areas of your relationships could benefit from more accountability and honesty?

9. Aligning Financial Decisions with Purpose

   How can you shift your financial decisions to align more closely with your true values and the kind of world you want to live in? What changes can you make today to start this alignment?

10. Being the Difference in Your Community

    What can you do in your local community to take radical responsibility and make a positive impact? How can you inspire others to do the same, creating a ripple effect of change?

REWRITE THE SCRIPT

Have you ever found yourself buried under a mountain of charges, dodging those relentless credit card statements, and dancing around the hard truths of your financial situation? Yeah, me too. Here's what I've learned: Reality has a way of catching up with us, no matter how fast we run.

We've all had those moments where sticking our heads in the sand seems easier than facing our financial fears head-on. It's playing ostrich—hoping our troubles will vanish if we just ignore them long enough. Here's what you must know: Facing your fears is the key to unlocking your financial freedom.

I was meeting with a client last week who is a classic Avoider Alice. She's approaching her thirtieth birthday and, despite her desire to travel the world and embrace her free spirit, the fear of being a failure in her parents' eyes keeps her from even looking at her money. She hired me because she was tired of avoiding her finances, but what we discovered together was eye-opening. It wasn't about the money at all—it was about the fear that she was letting her parents (and herself) down. That realization was a *big* aha moment for her.

She wasn't avoiding her money; she was avoiding her feelings. Our brains are really tricky this way. There are layers to our relationships with money that a budget alone won't fix. We can all be Avoider Alices when we feel afraid, unworthy, or like we aren't measuring up financially. My question for you today is: What are you avoiding? Even if you don't want to avoid it anymore but find yourself sticking your head in the sand, get curious about why that's happening.

I know that taking that nerve-racking first step isn't just about facing reality—it's about seizing your personal authority, having clarity on the real problem, and finding peace amid the chaos. And hey, a healthier bank balance doesn't hurt either.

Ready to rewrite your money story? It starts with one small action today. Dive into discovering your unique money personality. Transform your finances from a source of stress into your greatest asset. It's time to take the reins and make your money work for you.

REDEFINING SACRIFICE: LIVING A VISION-CENTERED LIFE

The word "sacrifice" has been overused and overplayed in personal finance. It's often a way to make someone feel ashamed or judged for their choices. Telling someone they must sacrifice to get ahead is disempowering and, frankly, oppressive.

Instead of feeling like you have to sacrifice to get ahead, try this:

1. Create a bold, heart-centered vision for your life.
2. Prioritize what truly matters to live out that vision.
3. Say yes to everything that aligns with your vision—remember, you get *one* life (as far as we know).

4. Focus your financial priorities so you can track progress and experience your vision coming to life.

This isn't about sacrifice; it's about living a vision-centered life. No sacrifice is necessary when you're living a life that's alive, filled with your vision, values, and priorities.

What does freedom mean to you? Just like feeling broke, freedom is a state of mind. How do you envision freedom for yourself? Would it mean spending money without hesitation? Booking a flight anywhere in the world without answering to anyone? Sending your child to a safe, quality school? These aren't the kinds of questions your financial adviser will ask, but they're the ones that matter.

Instead of relying on others for answers, let's start with a formula that connects you with your deepest desires.

BE INTENTIONAL

For a long time, I approached my business with a wing-it mentality. Relying on my natural talent and instincts allowed me to navigate through various situations, often leading to short-term successes. However, this approach came at a cost. Without a clear, intentional strategy, I found myself missing opportunities, making avoidable mistakes, and feeling a persistent sense of disconnection from my long-term goals.

My neuro-linguistic programming (NLP) training was a game changer. It provided me with a new roadmap—one that emphasizes the importance of intentionality in everything I do. I learned that by being deliberate in my actions, I could align my day-to-day efforts with my larger vision. Now, I'm committed to bringing that level of focus and intention into every aspect of my business. No more winging it—every move I make is purposeful and designed to move me closer to my goals.

FAKING IT UNTIL YOU MAKE IT DOESN'T WORK

For over two decades, I took the stage at countless events, relying on a mix of adrenaline and a fake-it-until-you-make-it mindset. Despite outward appearances of confidence, there were moments when I didn't feel worthy or adequately prepared. Just before stepping on stage, I'd tell myself, "Fuck it" as a way to push through the fear. I was unaware of how much more effective I could have been with proper preparation and a deeper sense of self-worth.

The truth is, I didn't know what I didn't know about preparation. But as I've grown and learned—especially through my NLP training—I've come to understand that vulnerability is not a weakness, but a superpower. It takes courage to show up authentically, and when I do, I'm able to connect with my audience on a deeper level. This authentic connection is what drives my success today. Faking it might get you by in the short term, but true, lasting success comes from being real, prepared, and vulnerable.

FEAR HAS HELD ME BACK

For much of my life, fear has been a silent but powerful force in my decision-making. I carried an unconscious fear of being judged, manipulated, or taken advantage of—a fear that influenced how I interacted with others, both personally and professionally. My unconscious mind was trying to protect me, but in doing so, it often held me back from forming deeper connections and seizing opportunities.

It wasn't until I started to delve into NLP that I realized how much this fear had been controlling me. Through the process, I learned to listen to my unconscious mind, to understand the messages it was sending, and to trust myself more fully. This journey has taught me the importance of setting healthy boundaries and not giving myself away in relationships or business. It was a difficult lesson, one I learned through some tough experiences, but I'm deeply grateful for it. Now, with this newfound understanding, I'm able to move forward with more confidence, clarity, and self-trust.

Last year alone, I invested over $60,000 in my personal and professional development. There were times I felt like I was coming unhinged, times I wanted to give up. But instead of crumbling under the pressure, I leaned in. I listened. I opened myself up to feedback. I had the courage to be wrong and the courage to ask for help.

I believe that the combination of investing in myself and having the courage to be real, open, and honest with myself was the stepping stone I needed to pave my path to success.

What was standing in my way? Me. But not anymore.

JOURNALING PROMPTS

Stop Budgeting, Start Living
Flip the Script

1. Identifying Avoidance Patterns

   Think about a time when you avoided dealing with a financial issue. What were the underlying feelings or fears driving that avoidance? How can you address these emotions to break the cycle?

2. Creating a Vision-Centered Life

   What is your bold, heart-centered vision for your life? How can you align your financial decisions with this vision to create a life that truly reflects your values and priorities?

3. Redefining Sacrifice

   How has the idea of sacrifice shown up in your financial life? How can you shift from a mindset of sacrifice to one of living with intention and purpose?

4. Exploring the Meaning of Freedom

   What does financial freedom mean to you? How can you start making financial choices today that move you closer to your vision of freedom?

5. Embracing Intentionality

   Reflect on a recent financial decision you made. Was it intentional and aligned with your long-term goals, or was it made on impulse? How can you bring more intentionality into your financial life?

6. Rejecting Fake It Until You Make It

   Think about a time when you relied on the fake-it-until-you-make-it mentality. How did that approach serve you, and what would have been different if you had embraced vulnerability and preparation instead?

7. Confronting Fear

   How has fear held you back in your financial or personal life? What can you do to confront this fear and move forward with more confidence and self-trust?

8. Investing in Yourself

   What areas of your life could benefit from personal or professional development? How can you invest in yourself to overcome obstacles and achieve your goals?

9. Rewriting Your Money Story

   If you could rewrite your money story, what would it look like? How can you take the first steps toward creating this new narrative in your financial life?

PART THREE
REDEFINING SUCCESS

. . . .

You are your best thing.
—*Toni Morrison*

MAKE IT
DEEPLY PERSONAL

Tear it all down—tear down the walls, tear down the limitations, tear down everything that's been holding you back. Only then can you build something new from a blank canvas. When I dove into my own work, I didn't fully grasp how profound the change would be. But let me tell you, it was a game changer. I experienced firsthand how the process of rewiring your mindset can transform the way you see the world.

Through the NLP breakthrough process, I was able to unravel the unconscious web I'd woven since childhood—a web that had been causing me pain for years. I realized that when my grandmother, who was my safe person, got sick and ended up in a home, losing her memory, I felt abandoned. As a teenager, I thought there was nothing I could do, and because I felt she was abandoned, I unconsciously abandoned myself. I was a good kid—no drugs, no alcohol, great grades, super involved in school. But then in college, I turned a corner into drugs, alcohol, and partying. I never knew why, until NLP helped me see that I was carrying deep pain from what happened with my grandma.

In one day, I was able to release and rewire how I think about my past. The things I had been looking at unconsciously changed. I felt relief, surprise, and a deep sense of forgiveness for myself and others. Twenty years of pain lifted, and I'm so grateful for this technology. And no, for the skeptics out there, I'm not in a cult. NLP works when you allow it to work and when it's used properly. It's the same technology Tony Robbins uses, rooted in neuroscience, and it's the foundation of so much transformational coaching.

You can heal your relationship with money.

Healing your relationship with money isn't just about crunching numbers or following a budget—it's about making it deeply, even intoxicatingly, personal. It's about transforming the way you think, feel, and interact with yourself, your life and others at the very core of who you are.

DISCOVER YOUR PURPOSE

Dare to dream. Dive deep into yourself. Fall madly in love with yourself. Do the inner work to uncover your true purpose, vision, and mission in life. This isn't just about money; it's about aligning your finances with what genuinely matters to you. When you know why, your financial decisions start to make sense, and money becomes a tool to help you fulfill your life's mission.

FORGIVE YOURSELF

We've all made choices out of fear and scarcity—choices that didn't align with our values or the future we want. It's time to forgive yourself for those decisions. Let go of the guilt and the shame. Understand that those choices were made with the knowledge and resources you had at the time. Forgiveness is the key to releasing the past and opening the door to a new financial future.

HEAL YOUR RELATIONSHIP WITH SPENDING

Spending isn't inherently good or bad. It's the meaning we attach to it that can cause problems. Instead of seeing spending as a negative, build a deep and meaningful relationship with it. Understand why you spend, what you're trying to achieve with each purchase, and how it aligns with your values. This process helps you reconcile your past financial habits and creates a healthier approach to spending.

LEARN THE POWER OF RESILIENCE

Perfection isn't the goal—progress is. You're human, and you will make mistakes along the way. The important thing is to learn from them, adapt, and keep moving forward. Resilience is about bouncing back from setbacks, learning from failures, and continuing to grow. This is how you become financially unstoppable—not by never falling, but by always getting back up.

Healing your relationship with money is a journey, not a destination. It's about continuous growth, self-discovery, and aligning your finances with the person you truly are.

It's time to change the narrative in personal finance. I'm on a mission to do just that. Because let's be honest—being successful doesn't always feel successful. There are bills to pay, people to pay, you've got to pay yourself, and you've got to make sure people pay you. Some days you'll have money, and some days you won't know where the money is going to come from. There will be risks worth taking, and many nights you'll question those risks. Accolades are few and far between, and even when they come, they're bittersweet. Some days you'll have to choose business over family, and most days you pray your family chooses you. There doesn't seem to be an end to the week, and some days you wish would never end. Success doesn't always feel successful, but I'm reminded writing this that there was a time when all I could dream about was being…me. And that's the magic of transformation!

Success is not a number. Broke is not a number. If that's the case, why do we put so damn much emphasis on numbers? Your relationship with money is a feeling, not a number. If you're going to start feeling happy and successful, you've got to realign with a vision and purpose in life that stretches beyond the numbers.

While I talk about what to do with your money in the playbook portion of this book, none of it matters if you don't have a clear, up-close, raw, and intimate relationship with why your money matters to you in the first place.

Most of my new clients can't even articulate what they want with their money. They don't know what they need to retire, they have no concept of how much they have to save, and they have no idea how to start waking up happy. Can you relate?

What makes you happy? Answering this question first is the best way to finally start feeling like you're on track to freedom.

To feel free, you need to build a trusting relationship with money and ensure that your emotional bank account is healthy. Think of a liability as an unfulfilled obligation between two parties. This perspective applies not just to finances, but to relationships as well.

Everyone's so busy talking about how to get rich. All I want to talk about is getting happy. There's no way to ever not be emotional with money. Our entire lives are lived one emotional choice after another.

What do you want for your life? (Emotional)

How do you want to live? (Emotional)

What's important to you? (Emotional)

Who do you want to marry? (Emotional)

What don't you want? (Emotional)

You can't make purely "logical" financial decisions. And for those of you who are building lives thinking this is possible, you need to challenge your concept of reality. Financial decisions are emotional decisions because we, as human beings, are emotional. It can't be any other way.

UNCOVER YOUR TRUTH

Have the courage to be radically fucking honest with yourself.

Melissa's story is a powerful reminder that real change begins with brutal honesty—especially with yourself. From the moment she was born, life threw every possible obstacle in her path. Both of her parents were entrenched in addiction, creating an environment of chaos and trauma that would deeply shape the course of Melissa's life. But it wasn't until she faced her truth head-on that she was able to break free from the cycles that had kept her trapped.

As a young child, Melissa was caught in the crossfire of her parents' tumultuous relationship. By the time she was two years old, her parents had divorced, and she found herself being raised predominantly by her father, a man struggling with his own demons of mental health and addiction. Without the guidance or support she needed, Melissa's early life was defined by neglect—by the time she was just seven or eight years old, she had already suffered severe dental problems as a direct result of that neglect.

The instability didn't stop there. Melissa was placed in foster care during a bitter custody battle between her parents, a situation that only further cemented her feelings of insecurity and confusion. By the time she went to live with her mother and stepfather around age eight, she was exposed to new layers of dysfunction, including gambling addictions and financial turmoil. Tasked with hiding her mom's credit card bills, Melissa learned early on that financial secrecy and mismanagement were the norm. This unhealthy relationship with money was being modeled for her, setting the stage for the patterns she would later repeat in her own life.

As Melissa grew older, she unknowingly continued the cycle. She got married young and handed over her entire paycheck to her husband, just as she had seen her mother do. By her mid-twenties, she found herself buried in debt, eventually filing for bankruptcy after trying to support herself and an unemployed partner. It was a stark reminder that the patterns we don't acknowledge and address will continue to control our lives.

But here's where Melissa's story takes a turn—a turn that required her to be brutally honest with herself. In her thirties, Melissa reached a breaking point. She could no longer ignore the deep-seated impact her childhood experiences were having on her life. In 2016, she enrolled in an NLP course, a decision that would force her to confront the subconscious beliefs driving her destructive behaviors. This was Melissa's moment of reckoning—she realized the glaring disconnect between her desires and her actions.

For the first time, she saw clearly how her past was dictating her present.

This radical honesty was the catalyst for change. Determined to break the cycles she had been trapped in, Melissa embarked on an intensive journey of healing and transformation. In 2019, she made the bold decision to pay off $40,000 in debt, taking on multiple jobs to do so. This was more than just a financial decision; it was a declaration that she was no longer willing to live in the shadows of her past.

But Melissa knew that financial freedom was only part of the equation. She also delved into somatic therapy, understanding that her trauma was not just in her mind, but held deep within her body and nervous system. Through this profound inner work, she was able to overcome the debilitating anxiety and panic attacks that had plagued her for years. Melissa emerged from this process with a newfound sense of self-trust, financial alignment, and a congruence between her mind, body, and values that she had never known before.

Melissa's story is a testament to the power of resilience, but more importantly, to the necessity of radical honesty with oneself. It's easy to coast through life, repeating the patterns that have been ingrained in us since childhood, but real transformation requires us to stop, look in the mirror, and ask the hard questions: Why am I doing this? What am I avoiding? What do I really want?

Until Melissa faced these questions, she was living a life dictated by the ghosts of her past. But once she confronted her truth, she was able to rewrite her story. Her journey serves as an inspiration to all of us, proving that no matter how daunting the circumstances, transformation is not just possible—it's inevitable when you're willing to be brutally honest with yourself and do the hard work of healing.

So, as you read this, ask yourself: What truth have you been avoiding? What parts of your life need a dose of radical honesty? Because the only way to truly change is to first face the truth, no matter how uncomfortable it may be. And in doing so, you'll find that the end of one story is just the beginning of a new one—one you get to write.

What's important about money to you? It's in there somewhere. Discovering your truth is like finding the key to a treasure chest you didn't even know you had. This isn't just a "nice-to-have" on your personal growth checklist—it's a nonnegotiable. When it comes to transforming your money mindset, uncovering your truth is where the real magic begins.

We live in a world that constantly tries to tell us who to be, what to want, and how to think. But none of that matters if it's not aligned with your truth. It's like wearing someone else's shoes—they might look great, but if they don't fit, you'll end up with blisters. And no one can run a marathon in ill-fitting shoes, especially not the marathon of life and financial success.

Your truth is your internal GPS. It guides you, keeps you grounded, and helps you navigate life's twists and turns with confidence. When you know your truth, you're not swayed by every trend, opinion, or piece of financial advice that comes your way. You have a clear sense of who you are, what you want, and why you're pursuing it.

Discovering your truth isn't a one-time event. It's a process, a journey of peeling back the layers of conditioning, expectations, and false beliefs that have built up over time. It's about getting real with yourself, asking the tough questions, and being brutally honest about what you find. And yes, it will be uncomfortable. That is a promise. But discomfort is often a sign that you're growing, stretching, moving closer to the life you're meant to live.

When it comes to your money mindset, your truth is the bedrock. It's the foundation upon which you build your financial goals, habits, and sense of worth. If your money mindset isn't rooted in your truth, it's like building a house on a shaky foundation. It might stand for a while, but eventually, the cracks will start to show.

Here's why it's nonnegotiable: When you operate from a place of truth, your actions align with your deepest values and desires. You're not just chasing money for the sake of it—you're pursuing financial freedom, security, or abundance because it aligns with who you truly are and what you genuinely want out of life. And that, my friends, is powerful. It's the kind of power that transforms not just your bank account, but your entire life.

So, if you're serious about transforming your money mindset, start by discovering your truth. Embrace it, honor it, and let it guide every decision you make. Because when you live from your truth, you're unstoppable. Your truth is your superpower—don't underestimate it, and definitely don't negotiate with it.

Dig deep, baby girl. You are worth it.

JOURNALING PROMPTS

Stop Budgeting, Start Living
You Are Your Best Thing

1. Uncovering Your Truth

   What is a deep truth about yourself that you've been avoiding? How might embracing this truth change the way you approach your life and your finances?

2. Healing Past Wounds

   Reflect on a painful experience from your past that still influences your financial decisions today. How can you begin to heal from this experience and reframe your relationship with money?

3. Defining Your Purpose

   What is your purpose in life? How does your financial situation align (or not align) with that purpose? What changes can you make to ensure your finances support your true mission?

4. Forgiving Yourself

   Think about a financial decision you regret. What were the circumstances that led to that decision, and how can you forgive yourself for it? What lessons have you learned that can guide your future choices?

5. Understanding Your Spending

   What emotions drive your spending habits? How can you create a more intentional relationship with money that aligns with your values and long-term goals?

6. Embracing Resilience

   Recall a time when you faced a financial setback. How did you respond, and what did you learn from the experience? How can you apply this resilience to future challenges?

7. Making It Personal

   What can you do to make your relationship with money deeply personal and meaningful? What steps can you take to ensure that your financial decisions reflect your true self and what matters most to you?

8. Challenging the Narrative of Success

   What does success mean to you, beyond financial numbers? How can you redefine success in a way that aligns with your values, emotions, and life goals?

9. Living Your Truth

   What would it look like to live fully in alignment with your truth? What changes would you need to make in your financial life, relationships, or daily habits to live more authentically?

10. Reflecting on Melissa's Story

    How does Melissa's story of radical honesty and transformation resonate with you? What parallels do you see in your own life, and how can you use her journey as inspiration for your own path of healing and growth?

EMOTIONAL BANK ACCOUNT

Relationships turn toxic when people consistently fail to meet their commitments. Can you relate? Just like in financial matters, when promises in a relationship aren't kept, things become toxic. Living a prosperous life isn't just about getting out of debt—it's about being healthy and whole in how you relate to yourself and others.

I've experienced this firsthand. After sixteen years of living with an alcoholic, I learned to set healthy boundaries with my ex-husband. His inability to fulfill his responsibilities as a husband and father was a liability in our relationship. Over time, that relationship became toxic and mirrored the dysfunction in our financial life. I had to take responsibility for allowing him to break his promises and for not setting healthy financial boundaries. It was tough, especially when we were raising a child together, dealing with his unstable employment due to his lack of sobriety, and managing the constant flow of money in and out of our household. The cycle of him charging on the credit card and me allowing it continued until I took radical responsibility for my choices.

When you're in relationships with people who don't keep their word, it creates toxicity.

> I encourage you to reflect on why you are where you are financially.

I encourage you to reflect on why you are where you are financially. Perhaps you're in debt because you're supporting someone who is draining your emotional bank account. Many parents come to me realizing that their debt is tied to a lack of healthy boundaries with their adult children. It's crucial to establish a healthy spending relationship with yourself and your family. I have a sixteen-year-old and a fourteen-year-old, and I'm already setting clear boundaries on what I'll pay for and what they are responsible for. As our kids grow, maintaining these boundaries is essential. I've seen countless parents with significant credit card debt because they haven't set those boundaries, and it doesn't feel good. When adult kids take more than they give and don't repay, it creates a cycle of enabling that's unhealthy for both the relationship and your finances. If this is you, you know what I'm talking about. This has nothing to do with shame. It's about being honest with yourself.

This isn't just about kids, either. Maybe you have an aging parent who isn't financially secure and is now relying on you. I've seen this with many clients who find themselves burdened with the financial responsibility of supporting a parent while trying to build their own lives.

Our emotional bank accounts and relationships can lead us off course financially. Let me be clear: You are not stupid, nor are you being totally irresponsible with your money. It's just that there's an emotional component at play. That's why, in my world, we emphasize healing your money mindset more than anything. Especially to get started. From a young age, you've developed habits and modeled financial behaviors, and if you don't have healthy financial boundaries with others, we can work on that. What's important is identifying the source of the problem so you can change it. It's an opportunity to audit your relationships and see how they are affecting your financial situation.

Let's consider Maya. She grew up poor, and as the second-oldest child, she had to step up when her older sister fell into addiction. Her family suffered, and Maya took on the responsibility of running the household. Now, twenty years later, she's stuck in a cycle of having money and then losing it—a cycle she desperately wants to break.

In one of our mindset sessions, I encouraged Maya to dream big. With tears in her eyes, she talked for twenty minutes about her dream of becoming a world-renowned photographer, owning a white Jeep and a black Suburban, living in Hawaii, and traveling the world. But when we returned to reality, I asked her what was truly important to her about money. Her answer?

Security.

Maya has a huge vision for her life, but she's stuck in a cycle of scarcity, rooted in the belief that she's responsible for saving her family whenever they're in need. If she wants to break this cycle, she has to be willing to confront her relationships and the decisions she made at a young age about her responsibility to her family.

Through our work together, Maya realized that her beliefs were deeply rooted in her unconscious. She wasn't raised around money, so she never learned how to keep it. When she did have money, there was always a family member asking for help. And she was afraid that her family would see her as one of "those people with money" who think they're better than everyone else. For Maya to have what she truly wants, she doesn't need a budget. She must set clear boundaries with her family and learn how to hold onto money. She needs to take care of her emotional bank account first.

It's not always easy to see when it's happening, but you have the opportunity to look at what may or may not be working in your relationships. You can get on a new path in life, and it starts with understanding where you are making your emotional investments. When your relationships are out of balance, it's the first place to look to recalibrate.

You can't afford toxic emotional bank accounts; no one can.

Toxic relationships have a direct correlation to your bank account.

This one's tough, but it's something I've learned the hard way: Not everyone deserves VIP access to you. This realization was a game changer for me. You can't give everyone in your life that level of access—it's simply not sustainable. It's time to identify your core people, and that might mean reevaluating some of your current relationships.

I remember a client who did the exercise I'm about to share with you. Afterward, she had a powerful revelation: Her adult children were the ones she had no boundaries with, and all her money was flowing to them. She was understandably upset, but she came back the next day and said, "Lisa, I've figured out why I'm struggling financially. It's these adult kids I keep supporting. And you know what? No Christmas for them this year." I was taken aback, but I got it. She realized the financial and emotional cost of always being the one to host, to buy the presents, to be the provider.

She decided to prioritize herself, which meant some tough conversations were coming her way. This is the kind of courage it takes to break free from debt, from toxic relationships, from anything holding you back. It's not just about crunching numbers; it's about examining the people around you. If you're not happy with your financial situation, it's on you to realign your circle.

Think about it—if you have a coworker who always drags you into gossip sessions when all you want is a quiet lunch, are they helping or hurting you? These distractions can derail your financial goals. Especially if you're someone who tends to give too much, it's crucial to assess who's in your life and whether they're contributing to your success.

My turning point came when I decided to get a divorce. That was the day I stood up for myself and said, "This isn't working anymore." But it wasn't just my marriage; I had to let go of other people too. I was spreading myself—and my money—too thin. Once I got clear on who my core people were, my entire financial life turned around, including my business.

So, let's start with building a trusting relationship with your money and making sure your core group is aligned with your financial goals. Have the courage to remove toxic people from your life, or at least adjust their access to you. Doing this will bring you more peace, freedom, and clarity than you can imagine.

So, who's in your core? These are the people you prioritize—your immediate family, your significant other (if those relationships are healthy), your spiritual guides, and your mentors.

For me, having coaches who could step in and help me tweak my life was crucial.

Now, here's your homework: Make a list of the top ten to fifteen people you spend the most time with.

Rate them plus or minus. It may feel harsh, but it's necessary.

For example, when I did this exercise a decade ago, my dad and I had a toxic relationship, and there was a lot of negativity. Over time, I healed myself, and then I healed that relationship. So, who are the liabilities in your life? Who takes more than they give? Do an audit, then talk it through with someone you trust. Identify what needs to change to improve your emotional and financial well-being.

I promise this is the best kind of audit you could ever do. It has nothing to do with numbers, and it will have a big impact on your life.

JOURNALING PROMPTS

Stop Budgeting, Start Living
Emotional Bank Account—Audit Time

1. Assessing Your Relationships

   Reflect on the top ten to fifteen people you spend the most time with. Who in your life adds to your emotional and financial well-being, and who might be draining it? How can you adjust these relationships to create a healthier balance?

2. Setting Boundaries

   Think about a relationship where you've struggled to set boundaries. What are the consequences of not setting those boundaries, both emotionally and financially? What steps can you take to establish healthier limits?

3. Understanding Your Emotional Bank Account

   Consider the emotional investments you've made in your relationships. Where have you overextended yourself, and how has this impacted your financial life? What changes can you make to ensure your emotional bank account stays healthy?

4. Healing Financial Toxicity

   Reflect on a time when a toxic relationship affected your finances. How did it impact your financial decisions, and what did you learn from the experience? How can you apply those lessons to your current relationships?

5. Identifying Core Relationships

    Who are the core people in your life that support your goals and well-being? How can you nurture these relationships while setting boundaries with those who may not be aligned with your financial and emotional health?

6. Forgiving Yourself

    Have you ever made financial sacrifices in a relationship that you later regretted? How can you forgive yourself for these choices and move forward with greater awareness and self-compassion?

7. Balancing Responsibility and Support

    How do you balance your responsibility to others with your own financial well-being? What boundaries can you set to ensure that you are not compromising your financial health for the sake of others?

8. Reflecting on Parental Influences

    Consider how your relationship with your parents or caregivers has influenced your financial decisions. Are there any patterns or beliefs you've inherited that you need to reassess?

9. Reevaluating Support for Adult Children

    If you have adult children, how do you support them financially? Are there areas where you need to set clear boundaries to protect your financial health and their independence?

10. Taking Radical Responsibility

How can you take radical responsibility for your financial life by auditing your relationships? What changes can you make today to improve your emotional and financial well-being?

BREAK THE GLASS CEILING

Radical responsibility changes the game, and this truth hits hardest when you realize that the person most often standing in our way is yourself. It's not entirely your fault— your financial set point and limiting beliefs deeply influence the decisions you make. But here's the deal: Until you fully own that it's you who are limiting your progress, you can't move forward. This is why you must look inward first.

You are underearning. Women chronically underearn. According to recent studies, women in the United States still earn about eighty-two cents for every dollar earned by men, and this gap is even wider for women of color. When women come to me, the last thing I tell them to do is budget. The first focus is on the top line—what they're earning.

If we continue to allow others to control our financial futures, we will stay on this same path, and we simply cannot afford this anymore. We can no longer allow anyone to pay us less or treat us as less—starting with ourselves.

Let me tell you a story. My dad never made more than $60,000 a year. By the time I hit thirty and started earning

$55,000, I couldn't see how life could get much better. I thought I had made it! That was my self-imposed ceiling, and it took meeting new people and having conversations to realize that this ceiling was an artificial cap, created by my own limiting expectations.

But it wasn't until I was going broke that I had to truly confront this. I spent so much time pointing the finger at everyone else—my husband, my business partners, my family—but never at myself. In 2015, my coach asked me how much I wanted to make that year, and I confidently said $30,000. She looked at me and said, "Angie, why would you ever limit yourself this way?" That was a big fat awakening. I realized that I had been the one limiting myself all along—and we all do it in some way or another. The key to breaking through this is by taking radical responsibility and then doing the work to identify the ways that you are limiting yourself.

Our relationship with money is one that lasts our entire life. Any time invested in building good habits and enhancing that relationship now will continue to pay off for years. That's why there's no better time than now to cast aside our budget-focused mindsets and release ourselves from the guilt associated with spending. Budgets often pull us right back into living under the ceilings we've created, keeping us financially small and stuck in a scarcity mindset rather than one of abundance.

In reality, no one is forcing us to live this way. We create our own boxes and decide to stay in them. But it doesn't feel that way, does it? And that's how we stay stuck—we make it everyone else's fault but our own. If you want something new in your life, you are the one responsible for creating it.

Take Lacie, for example. She knew nothing but financial fear, scarcity, and volatility. It's the life she was born into. By the time we met, she was completely shut down and numbed out. She had a child with her partner, and they kept their finances completely separate. They never talked numbers. He had no idea about her debt, student loans, or spending habits, and she had no clue where his money went—all she knew was that he paid the mortgage. She had no real relationship with her money. She paid her bills, her credit card minimums, and after that, she had no idea where her money was going.

This isn't a story about what a failure Lacie is. In fact, she's brilliant. She's an incredible mom with a heart of gold. But Lacie grew up on food stamps, in a family riddled with alcoholism. As a single mom at twenty-one, she repeated the cycle of poverty she grew up in. The difference is that Lacie grew up in a time where women had financial options that her mom never did. So she did what many millennial women are doing today—she took out student loans, put herself through a master's program, and tried to get out of her small town to provide a better life for her daughter. But money was always a matter of survival for her. She had never enjoyed money, much less thought that she could. Money was scary and elusive, and she avoided her financial obligations like the plague. She didn't know any different.

It wasn't her fault. Her financial set point of scarcity, fear, and avoidance started at a very young age. She had no role models of financial stability or ease. No one taught her how to make financial decisions. All she knew was that if she wanted anything in life, it was going to be a struggle to get it. This was the framework of her relationship with money—addiction, feast and famine, and despair. And her husband deepened this well of shame every time he tried to force her into budgeting.

Lacie struggled for years, and when it came time to choose her career path, she knew she wanted to help others avoid the same struggle. So, she took out more student loans, went back to school, and became a social worker. But despite her best efforts, she remained stuck in that cycle of financial instability.

The first exercise I had Lacie do was a financial inventory. If she wanted to reach a new destination with her money, she had to know where she was starting from. This was a huge wake-up call—she realized she was $7,000 in the red every month. She had been using credit cards as a crutch, avoiding the realities of her situation, and it was bankrupting her.

But here's where the magic happened: Lacie took responsibility and got to work. It didn't take long for me to see how motivated and brilliant she really was. We put simple systems in place for her to track her money, and then we shifted focus to emotionally rewiring and healing her money mindset.

With support, Lacie learned how to have tough conversations with her partner, who was unintentionally throwing their joint finances out of balance. He made significantly more money than she did, but they were still splitting expenses fifty-fifty. Lacie renegotiated that division, releasing a lot of the pent-up anxiety and fear she had around money. These changes helped Lacie not only stop the $7,000 monthly bleed, but also get out of debt entirely.

After working with me for several years, Lacie now manages finances for her entire household. She found the courage to leave a job she hated and has taken dream trips with her family. She's transformed her life and relationship with her finances so completely that she no longer needs me as a coach—a win for both of us! When Lacie's financial life stabilized, her whole life upgraded.

If you truly believe you don't have any money, you're going to operate from a place of scarcity and fear across all aspects of your life. That's not the future I wanted for Lacie, and it's not the reality I want for you. Instead, I want you to see that if you have any income at all, you have money. Maybe you don't have as much as you'd like, or you're not where you want to be yet, but you still have money. The power to break through that self-imposed glass ceiling is within you—starting with taking radical responsibility for your financial choices.

If you picked up this book, it's because you're ready to make some much-needed changes in your life. You're ready to take control of your financial future, to break through the limitations that have been holding you back, and to create a life of abundance and fulfillment. You're in the right place.

Remember, the journey begins with you. The moment you take radical responsibility for your life, your finances, and your future, you unlock the power to transform everything. You have what it takes to break the glass ceiling, to earn what you're truly worth, and to live the life you've always dreamed of. This is your time. Let's make it happen.

JOURNALING PROMPTS

Stop Budgeting, Start Living
Busting Through, Baby

1. Identifying Your Financial Ceiling

    Reflect on your current income and financial situation. What self-imposed limitations or beliefs might be holding you back from earning more? How can you begin to challenge and break through these ceilings?

2. Taking Radical Responsibility

    Think about a time when you blamed external circumstances or other people for your financial situation. How can you take full responsibility for your financial choices moving forward?

3. Understanding Your Financial Set Point

    What financial beliefs or set point did you inherit from your family or upbringing? How have these influenced your earning potential and financial decisions? What new beliefs can you adopt to create a more abundant financial future?

4. Redefining Your Worth

    How do you currently perceive your worth in terms of earning potential? What steps can you take to ensure that you are being compensated fairly for your skills, experience, and contributions?

5. Confronting Financial Realities

    What financial realities have you been avoiding? How can you face these realities head-on and begin taking actionable steps to improve your financial situation?

6. Building Confidence in Negotiations

    How confident do you feel when negotiating your salary or fees? What strategies can you employ to strengthen your negotiation skills and advocate for the compensation you deserve?

7. Healing Your Money Mindset

    Reflect on any negative emotions or fears you associate with money. How can you begin to heal your relationship with money and shift to a mindset of abundance and possibility?

8. Creating a Vision for Your Financial Future

    What is your vision for your financial future? How does this vision align with your values and long-term goals? What steps can you take today to start turning this vision into reality?

9. Recognizing Your Value

    Think about the value you bring to your work, business, or community. How can you better communicate and leverage this value to increase your earning potential and financial success?

10. Taking Action

What is one concrete action you can take today to start breaking through your financial glass ceiling? How will this action contribute to your overall financial growth and success?

PART FOUR
LIVING YOUR HIGHEST PURPOSE

....

Money isn't happiness.
Happiness is the only way to happiness.

HELL YES

The journey to living your highest purpose is not about finding joy in every moment, but about being radically honest with yourself, confronting the hard truths, and making decisions that align with your deepest values. Joy Hoover's story is a powerful example of what it means to take control of your life by being brutally honest about where you are, what you want, and what needs to change.

Joy grew up in a small town in Michigan, the youngest of seven children. Her life was far from easy. Both of her parents were full-time evangelical pastors, juggling multiple jobs to support their large family. Money was always tight, and the scarcity of it cast a long shadow over her upbringing. Her father, who had known poverty intimately, harbored a deep-seated resentment toward wealth, while her mother, who had experienced a more comfortable upbringing, longed for things that her father couldn't provide. This tension created an environment where money was associated with fear, sacrifice, and unmet desires.

From an early age, Joy knew she wanted more for herself, even if she wasn't exactly sure what "more" would look like.

By sixteen, she had graduated from high school and moved to Grand Rapids, Michigan, to pursue her dreams. But dreams, as Joy soon discovered, don't come without their own set of challenges. She met her future husband, Phil, and together they embarked on a life that would test their resilience in ways they never expected.

After getting married, Joy and Phil moved to California so Joy could attend fashion school. They were young and inexperienced in managing money, and soon found themselves struggling just to get by. Living in a cramped apartment with a roommate, they took on side jobs, participated in clinical trials, and even donated plasma to make ends meet. But despite their hustle, the financial pressure became too much, and they eventually moved back to Michigan, burdened with debt and uncertain about their future.

Back in Michigan, Joy and Phil made a critical decision—they were going to take control of their financial lives. This wasn't just about budgeting or cutting back on expenses; it was about being brutally honest with themselves about the choices they had made and the changes they needed to make. They reassessed their priorities, made sacrifices, and began to pay down their debt. This wasn't an easy process, but it was a necessary one—a turning point that would set the stage for everything that followed.

"IF IT'S NOT A HELL YES, IT'S A HELL NO"—JOY HOOVER

Today, Joy is a force of nature. She's the founder of Esoes Cosmetics, a company that was born from a simple yet profound idea that came to her while coloring with her five-year-old daughter. When her daughter suggested they do something with lipstick, Joy's curiosity was piqued. She began researching and discovered that there were no cosmetic products on the market addressing the critical issues of domestic and sexual violence. This realization sparked the creation of ESOES Cosmetics—a product line that provides not just beauty, but safety. One of the products even includes a lipstick with built-in safety features like a Bluetooth button that can connect to an app, providing customizable safety options.

But Esoes Cosmetics is more than just a business; it's a movement. Joy's vision is to empower women by giving them the tools they need to protect themselves while also providing employment opportunities and financial support to survivors.

It's a bold and ambitious mission, but if anyone can bring it to life, it's Joy.

What makes Joy's story so compelling isn't just her success but her willingness to be radically honest with herself about where she started and what she needed to do to change. She grew up in a family where money was a constant source of stress and fear and faced significant financial challenges as a young adult, yet she was able to transform those experiences into a mission that's making a real difference in the world.

Joy's journey teaches us that real transformation begins with radical honesty. It's about looking at your life and asking the hard questions: What isn't working? What am I avoiding? What do I really want? It's only when you're willing to confront the truth that you can begin to make meaningful changes.

In one of my recent conversations with Joy, she shared a quote that resonated deeply with me: "You can't hate your body into a body that you love." The same is true when it comes to money—you can't hate your financial situation into a relationship that you love. You have to do the work. Avoiding your emotions and your money at the same time adds up to a life of frustration and disappointment.

In every journey of transformation, there comes a pivotal moment when you must have the courage to say yes to the things in your life that you love the most. On the flip side of that, you must have the courage to say no to anything that does not feel right or good to you. The first step to healing is recognizing the wounds that need to be healed, and this requires a willingness to be brutally honest with yourself.

It's not easy, but it's essential for true growth and renewal.

Willingness is the gateway to change. It's the internal shift that says, "I am ready to see the truth, no matter how difficult it may be." This willingness is an act of self-love, a declaration that you are worth the effort and discomfort that comes with growth.

The journey of healing is not linear. It requires patience, persistence, and a deep commitment to yourself. As you confront your darkness, you may feel overwhelmed or tempted to turn back. But it's through this very confrontation that you discover your strength and resilience.

Joy Hoover's journey exemplifies this path. Her willingness to confront her past and the traumas she endured allowed her to transform her pain into a powerful mission with Esoes Cosmetics. By facing her darkness, she found the strength to create change not only in her life, but in the lives of countless others.

There is a profound light on the other side of our darkness. It's the light of self-acceptance, freedom, and empowerment. When you have the courage to face your shadows, you also discover your inner light—the aspects of yourself that are resilient, loving, and capable of immense growth.

As you read this, ask yourself: What truth have you been avoiding? What parts of your life need a dose of radical honesty?

Because the only way to truly change is to first face the truth, no matter how uncomfortable it may be. When you do, you'll find that the end of one story is just the beginning of a new one—one that you get to write.

Believing in yourself is the most important part of every journey you take.

Trust in action means that you trust you are on the right path, and you take action to show it.

Trust that you're making the right decisions, that you have the right systems, and that you're having the right conversations. Even if progress is slow at first, all of this moves you in the right direction.

Money has its job and its function in our lives; there's no getting around that. It ebbs and flows just like electricity, and if you're not paying attention to how strong the connection is, it could short-circuit at any time. Feeling like a hot mess with your finances? In debt up to your eyeballs? Totally winging it? Is that trust, or is that fear? Let's choose trust instead. Let's choose to take clear steps, make conscious changes, and trust that the financial life you dream of is possible.

Let's choose to say yes to more of what feels right and makes us feel good.

The power is in your hands. Right here, right now, you have the courage to trust that you are enough as you are, and that your value isn't tied to how perfectly you can orchestrate your life. The real strength lies in facing that fear, letting go of the need to control, and allowing yourself to experience life in all its messy, unpredictable glory. This is where true growth happens. This is where you find the courage to live a life that's richer, more meaningful, and authentically yours.

JOURNALING PROMPTS

Stop Budgeting, Start Living
Say "Hell Yes" More

1. Radical Honesty

    What truths about your life or financial situation have you been avoiding? How can you begin to face these truths with radical honesty?

2. Identifying Your "Hell Yes"

    What are the things in your life that make you feel a resounding "hell yes"? How can you prioritize these and say no to what doesn't align with your deepest values?

3. Facing Your Fears

    Reflect on a fear that has been holding you back. How can you confront this fear head-on and move toward a life that feels more authentic and fulfilling?

4. Trusting Yourself

    In what areas of your life do you struggle to trust yourself? How can you begin to build more trust in your decisions, actions, and overall direction?

5. Healing Old Wounds

    Consider a past experience or relationship that still affects you today. What steps can you take to heal from this and move forward with a sense of freedom and empowerment?

6. Defining Your Values

   What are your core values, and how do they influence your decisions? How can you ensure that your financial and personal choices align with these values?

7. Letting Go of Control

   Where in your life do you feel the need to control outcomes? How can you practice letting go and trusting the process, even when things feel uncertain?

8. Embracing Pleasure

   What are the things in your life that bring you pleasure? If you were not afraid, what would you do more of? What do you wish you could do more of?

9. Saying No to What Doesn't Serve You

   What areas of your life are currently draining your energy or resources? How can you start saying no to these to make more room for what truly matters?

10. Taking Inspired Action

    What is one action you can take today that feels like a "hell yes"? How will this action bring you closer to living a life that aligns with your true self?

TRUSTING YOURSELF WITH MONEY

Laying the groundwork for a trusting relationship with money isn't just important—it's the bedrock of everything you want financially. Think of it like constructing a house: You wouldn't start with the roof, right? Unless you want it all to come crashing down. Trust is your foundation, and without it, you might as well be building on quicksand.

Now, trust isn't just something that shows up unannounced like a distant relative at a family reunion. Nope, it comes after you've wrestled with your intentions and your purpose for money, really gotten into the ring with them. Let's be real: Our money is tangled up in every single decision we make, from the daily coffee splurge to the big investment decisions. You can't have a trusting relationship with money until you've got a trusting relationship with yourself—and that requires some serious soul-searching.

Trust in action is like getting that validation stamp on your passport to financial freedom. It's showing, through your behavior, that what you believe is actually true. If you believe you're worthy of a better financial life (and let's be honest, you are), then trust in action looks like tracking in a way that suits your unique money personality, organizing your finances, and following up regularly on things so they don't bite you in the ass. If you believe you can do this—even if you're still figuring out the how, trust in action looks like asking for help (yes, it's okay to ask for directions!) or finding a community that's got your back while you're on this journey.

How do you start making trust a reality in your life? Zip up your wetsuit, because we're taking a deep dive.

Let's take a closer look at the steps you need to take to really build a trusting relationship with your money. Remember, action takers are moneymakers! There are clear steps to make this happen, but it all starts with believing in yourself enough to actually take those steps. Being proactive isn't just a good idea—it's a necessity.

BUILDING A TRUSTING RELATIONSHIP WITH MONEY STARTS HERE

Addressing the relationships we have with money is often the first place I start when working with new clients. It's fundamental. If you can strengthen each piece of the five-pillar framework I call **TRUST**, you'll be well on your way to transforming your money mindset—and your life.

Tracking: Know Where You Stand

Tracking is like having a heart-to-heart with your money. Forget the B word (budgeting). Tracking is all about understanding where you are, financially speaking, and taking responsibility for every dollar that comes in and goes out. I remember when I first started tracking my expenses; it felt like I was shining a spotlight on all those little "innocent" purchases that somehow added up to a big dent in my bank account. The daily lattes, the spontaneous Amazon orders—guilty as charged. But here's the thing: Once I started tracking, I gained clarity. I knew exactly where my money was going, and that awareness alone gave me the power to make smarter decisions. Tracking isn't about restriction; it's about taking control and setting the stage for growth.

Return on Investment: Find the Value

Most people don't think about the value generated by their everyday purchases—they just see the money leaving their account and feel a pang of guilt. But what if I told you that spending doesn't have to be a shameful experience? When I first started focusing on the return on investment (ROI) of my spending, everything changed. For example, I used to feel bad about spending money on a high-quality meal out. But when I reframed it as an investment in my well-being, my enjoyment, and even my creativity (because let's be honest, a great meal can spark some serious inspiration), the guilt disappeared. Now, before any purchase, I ask myself, "What's the value of this to me?" It's a game changer that shifts the focus from guilt to financial intention.

Understand Your Why: Dig Deep

This is where the rubber meets the road. Understanding your why is like having a GPS for your financial life. Without it, you're just wandering aimlessly, spending money without a real sense of purpose. I've always believed that a budget is a tool for restriction, but knowing your why gives you the freedom to spend in alignment with your true goals. For instance, I once had a client who was struggling to save money. It wasn't until we dug deep into her motivations that she realized her true why was to create financial security for her children's future. That realization made saving less of a chore and more of a mission. Your why fuels your fire and gives you the drive to stick to your financial plans—even when the going gets tough.

Systems: Set Yourself Up for Success

Winging it might work for karaoke night, but it's not a winning strategy for managing your finances. Systems are the backbone of any successful financial plan. Take my three-account system, for instance. It's a simple, yet effective way to harness your money and use it to its full potential. I have one account for daily expenses, another for savings, and a third for investments. This system has not only helped me stay organized, but also allowed me to grab new opportunities as they come up. Think of systems as your financial blueprint—they keep you on track and ensure you're making the most of your resources. And trust me, once you have a system in place, you'll wonder how you ever managed without it.

Tools: Leverage Technology for Easy Wins

Let's talk about tools—your secret weapons in the financial game. We live in a time of incredible technological innovation, and if you're not taking advantage of it, you're missing out. Gone are the days of paper ledgers and manual expense tracking (thank goodness!) Nowadays, you can log into your bank account with one click and see exactly where your money is going. For me, finding the right tools was a game changer. I started using an app that not only tracks my spending, but also categorizes it, making it easy to see where I might be overdoing it (hello, dining out). These tools aren't your enemies; they're your assistants, making life easier and more efficient. And here's a pro tip: If a tool isn't working for you, don't be afraid to ditch it. There's no one size fits all when it comes to managing money—find what works for you and run with it.

Each piece of the TRUST framework is essential to building a strong, healthy relationship with money. It's not just about managing your finances; it's about taking control of your life. When you understand where you're starting from, focus on the value of your spending, dig deep into your motivations, set up systems for success, and leverage the right tools, you're not just changing your money mindset—you're transforming your entire life.

Trust in Action

Trust in action is all about participation. It's about believing you've got what it takes to achieve your dreams and build a secure financial future. But belief is just part of the equation. You also need to trust that the actions you take—like using systems, tools, and tracking—will lead to the results you want. Giving your financial goals the TLC they deserve is your responsibility to the trust you've placed in your dreams.

Meet Eileen. We crossed paths years ago at a networking event in a bowling alley in Las Vegas (true story). At that time, she was just starting to dip her toes into the world of real estate. Today, she's the powerhouse behind a six-figure brokerage, but her journey to success was anything but straightforward. Eileen's story is one of grit, resilience, and the courage to rewrite the script she was handed about money and self-worth.

Eileen grew up in an abusive family, where survival meant keeping your head down and doing whatever it took to stay out of trouble. The environment was harsh, filled with fear, control, and the constant threat of violence. There was no room for vulnerability, no space for dreams. Life was about enduring, not thriving. The messages she received were clear: Don't ask for help, don't show weakness, and don't expect anything to change.

By the time Eileen was seventeen, she knew she had to get out. The home that was supposed to be her refuge had become a prison, and she realized that if she didn't leave, she might never escape the cycle of abuse and control. So, with little more than sheer determination, Eileen walked away from everything she knew, stepping into the unknown with nothing but the hope that there had to be something better out there.

But leaving wasn't the end of her struggles—it was just the beginning. Eileen had to confront the deep-seated beliefs that had been drilled into her since childhood. She had been raised to believe that needing help was a sign of failure, that asking for support meant you were weak. These limiting beliefs followed her into adulthood, shaping her relationship with money, success, and even her sense of self-worth.

Life, however, has a way of forcing us to confront the very things we try to avoid. As Eileen dove deeper into real estate, she found herself facing financial challenges that threatened to derail her dreams. The road to building her brokerage was filled with setbacks and obstacles, but the biggest battle she fought was within herself. She had to learn to trust her instincts, to believe that she was capable of more than just surviving—she was capable of thriving.

Eileen will tell you that she wasn't the type to ask for help. It went against everything she had been taught. But as the challenges mounted, she realized that if she was going to break free from the chains of her past, she had to do things differently. Accepting help didn't mean she had failed; it meant she was willing to grow. It meant she was strong enough to acknowledge her weaknesses and brave enough to seek out the support she needed to overcome them.

Slowly but surely, Eileen began to rewrite her beliefs about money, success, and herself. She faced her financial challenges head-on, made tough decisions, and took the necessary actions to fix what was broken. Each step forward was a step away from the girl who had once felt trapped and powerless, and a step closer to the woman she was becoming—confident, empowered, and in control of her own destiny.

Today, Eileen's brokerage is thriving, a testament to her resilience and the hard work she's put in over the years. But more than that, it's a testament to the power of believing in yourself, even when the world has taught you not to. Eileen's story is a reminder that no matter where you start, no matter how dark your past may be, you have the power to rewrite your script. You have the power to break free, to ask for help, and to create a life that's not just about survival, but about true success.

Real estate agents know the struggle: One month you're flush with cash, the next month you're wondering if you can pay the bills. Eileen realized that, while she was great at tracking and balancing, her credit card debt was dragging her down. The act of taking cash out hurt more than swiping a card, so she racked up debt. But trust in action for Eileen meant facing that debt, feeling the shame, and fixing it step by step. And fix it she did—she's paid off nearly $100,000 in credit card debt while growing her successful business.

Eileen's story is a testament to trust in action. She didn't let her debt control her—she took control. You can hear more about her journey on my *Real Money* podcast.

Building real relationships, including a relationship with money, is based on trust. And trust, my friends, is the only way.

JOURNALING PROMPTS

Stop Budgeting, Start Living
Time to Trust

1. Reflecting on Trust

    What does trust mean to you when it comes to your relationship with money? How has your trust in yourself influenced your financial decisions in the past?

2. Tracking Your Finances

    How comfortable are you with tracking your expenses? What emotions arise when you think about where your money goes? How can you begin to track your finances in a way that feels empowering rather than restrictive?

3. Identifying Value in Spending

    Think about a recent purchase. What value did it bring to your life? How does understanding the value of your spending change the way you view your finances?

4. Understanding Your Why

    Why is financial freedom important to you? What deeper goals and desires motivate your financial decisions? How can connecting with your why help you make more aligned choices?

5. Building Systems

    What systems do you currently have in place to manage your money? Are they working for you, or do they need adjustment? How can you create or improve systems that support your financial goals?

6. Leveraging Tools

    What financial tools or apps do you use to manage your money? Are they helping you, or do you feel overwhelmed by them? How can you better leverage technology to simplify and improve your financial life?

7. Facing Financial Fears

    What financial fears have you been avoiding? How can you confront these fears and take steps to build a more trusting relationship with your money?

8. Taking Action

    What small action can you take today to demonstrate trust in yourself and your financial decisions? How will this action move you closer to your financial goals?

9. Evaluating Relationships

    How do your relationships (with yourself, others, and money) impact your financial well-being? Are there any toxic relationships or habits that you need to address to improve your financial health?

10. Embracing Resilience

When faced with financial setbacks, how do you typically respond? How can you build resilience and continue to trust yourself even when things don't go as planned?

EMBRACING YOUR SHADOW

Think back to being seven years old again. That's when the foundation of your financial identity started to form, shaped heavily by the adults and the environment around you. Those snippets of conversations about money from your parents, the subtle cues from your teachers—all of those experiences have woven intricate patterns into your psyche. Kids are incredibly perceptive; they pick up every financial whisper and shout, storing these insights away for the future.

This early conditioning evolves into a complex tapestry of inherited traits and learned behaviors. Each layer of conditioning we peel back reveals more about our financial beliefs and experiences. However, this journey of self-discovery often uncovers some less-than-pleasant truths—old, nagging beliefs that whisper, "I'm not worthy," "I can't do it," or "Success isn't meant for me." These are the voices that can really hold us back.

Did you know our brains process about sixty-six thousand thoughts each day? And here's the kicker—two-thirds of these are negative. That's a whole lot of pessimism clouding our judgment, especially around money. It's especially pronounced for women. Research, like the 2020 US Bank Women and Wealth Insights Study, shows that many women connect financial planning with fear, anxiety, and inadequacy more than men do.

How do we begin to reconcile this? To start, recognizing that these deep-seated negative thoughts actually exist is the first step. They're not just minor worries; they're powerful beliefs that influence how we manage money and see ourselves in every aspect of life.

A DEEP DIVE WITH ROSALYN ACOSTA

Recently on my podcast, I had a conversation with Rosalyn Acosta, a Reiki master and shamanic energy medicine practitioner. We explored how our root chakras and the broader chakra system could be influencing our financial behaviors. An out-of-balance root chakra might show itself in hoarding money or perpetually feeling financially insecure. Through energy work like Reiki, Rosalyn helps to balance these energies, paving the way for healthier financial habits and mindsets.

IGNORING THE WORK HAS CONSEQUENCES

Let me level with you—if we skip out on shadow and healing work, we're ignoring the trauma and emotional experiences stored in our bodies. For an overview of what shadow work is, see the Appendix. It's like being aware of our flaws but doing nothing about them. When we don't address these issues, we risk perpetuating unhealthy family patterns—fear, scarcity, anxiety—that have been passed down through generations.

Instead of trying to eradicate these shadowy parts of ourselves, what would be possible if we brought them into the light and learned from them? Why don't we?

Sometimes, it feels really heavy. I get that. I really, really do. And, it's already heavy. Learning how to slowly lean into our pain is one of the most courageous things we can do for ourselves.

What healing requires is for us to be honest with ourselves, face our fears, and recognize them as integral parts of our whole being. This isn't about battling our darker sides; it's about understanding and integrating them to move forward genuinely.

Combining energy work with financial healing shows us how our spiritual and energetic states directly impact our financial health. It's about much more than just fixing our budgets—it's about aligning our entire being, from the energy we carry to the money we manage.

Imagine if we keep ignoring our deeper issues. We're essentially stumbling through life blindfolded. It's time to remove the blindfolds, confront our shadows, and light up our paths to financial and emotional freedom. Let's transform not just bank accounts, but our entire beings. Let's live fully, authentically, and with all the financial wisdom we deserve.

Here's the deal: Embracing our shadows involves a deep dive into those parts of ourselves we might not be so proud of—the fears, the doubts, the insecurities. But it's also about recognizing the strength, resilience, and wisdom that come from facing those shadows. This process isn't just healing; it's empowering. It's about taking everything life throws at you and using it to build a stronger, more confident you.

Picture a woman, let's call her Clara, who sees her shadow as a dark, sprawling forest—too vast, too dense, too intimidating to ever venture into. Instead of exploring it, she stays clear, insisting on living in perpetual sunshine, where everything appears bright and unblemished (we can also call this a form of toxic positivity). This denial, this refusal to acknowledge the darker parts of her existence, leads her to a superficial life, adorned with forced smiles and relentless positivity. Yet, beneath that shiny exterior, Clara is crumbling.

As the years roll by, the weight of unaddressed emotions and unresolved issues starts manifesting physically. Chronic pain becomes her constant companion, a tangible reminder of the shadows she's ignored. To cope, she finds herself slipping into a numbing routine—painkillers for the body, mindless entertainment for the spirit. Her job feels like a prison, her relationships shallow. Her life, once a vibrant canvas, now a dull, monotonous gray.

One dreary morning, Clara catches her reflection in the mirror. The fatigue in her eyes is palpable, the disillusionment written all over her face. She's sick of herself, sick of the pain, sick of the emptiness. It's this moment of raw, unfiltered truth that sparks a desperate need for change.

Faced with her reality, Clara decides to brave the forest of her shadows. She reaches out for help. She begins her journey with an energy healer, someone skilled at navigating the complex landscapes of the soul, much like Rosalyn Acosta. This healer's approach, which seamlessly integrates Reiki and precise shamanic techniques, helps Clara confront and begin to heal her pain.

Working with her shadows, Clara learns to embrace not just the pain, but the lessons it brings. She discovers that her chronic ailments are not just random misfortunes but are deeply tied to emotional blockages and past traumas. As she starts addressing these, not only does her physical pain begin to subside, but her entire outlook on life shifts.

She finds a new job—one that resonates with her passions and gives her a sense of purpose. Her relationships grow deeper, more meaningful. She starts enjoying life's simple pleasures again, finding joy in moments she would have ignored before. The energy work opens her up to a new realm of possibilities, where challenges are met with resilience and growth rather than fear and avoidance.

Clara's journey into her shadow forest wasn't easy. It required her to face fears, revisit old wounds, and acknowledge parts of herself she had long denied. But the transformation was profound. She not only healed her physical pain, but also discovered a richer, more authentic way to live. Her life, once governed by denial and superficial positivity, now thrives on genuine self-acceptance and deep, personal fulfillment.

Her story is a powerful testament to the transformative impact of embracing our shadows. By acknowledging and integrating these darker parts of ourselves, we can overcome financial instability and deep-seated emotional and physical issues. It's about healing holistically, aligning every aspect of our beings with our truest selves.

Let Clara's journey inspire you. If you find yourself tired of the pain, weary of the facade, or just sick of feeling stuck, remember it's never too late to turn to your shadows and ask what they're trying to tell you. Embrace them, learn from them, and watch as they illuminate a path to a life filled with more joy, more purpose, and more fulfillment than you ever thought possible. This is your call to action—dive into your shadow, heal your pain, and reclaim the life you deserve. Let's embark on this transformative journey together, stepping into our power and rewriting our stories with courage and authenticity.

JOURNALING PROMPTS

Stop Budgeting, Start Living
Shadow Play

1. Reflecting on Childhood Influences

    Think back to when you were seven years old. What are your earliest memories of money, and how did the adults around you talk about or handle it? How have these early experiences shaped your current financial beliefs and behaviors?

2. Identifying Negative Thoughts

    What recurring negative thoughts do you have about money or success? How do these thoughts affect your decisions and actions in your financial life?

3. Facing Your Shadows

    What aspects of yourself or your financial behaviors have you been avoiding? Why do you think you've been avoiding them, and how might confronting these shadows help you grow?

4. Exploring Your Shadow's Impact

    How have your unaddressed fears, doubts, or insecurities influenced your financial decisions? In what ways have they held you back from achieving your goals?

5. Healing Through Awareness

    What emotions or traumas are tied to your financial behaviors? How can acknowledging and understanding these emotions help you heal and transform your relationship with money?

6. The Role of Energy in Financial Health

    How do you think your spiritual or energetic state influences your financial well-being? Have you noticed any patterns where emotional or physical imbalances impact your financial health?

7. Integrating Your Shadow

    What lessons can you learn from the darker parts of yourself? How can you integrate these lessons into your life to create a more balanced and authentic approach to money?

8. Confronting Physical Manifestations

    Have you experienced any physical symptoms, such as chronic pain or fatigue, that you believe are connected to unresolved emotional or financial issues? What steps can you take to address these underlying causes?

9. Rewriting Your Story

    Imagine yourself as the protagonist in your own story. How can you rewrite the narrative to include healing, growth, and a deeper understanding of your financial and emotional shadows?

10. Creating a New Path Forward

What new practices or actions can you take to embrace your shadow and move toward a healthier relationship with money and yourself? How will you hold yourself accountable on this journey?

THE JOURNEY OF HEALING

We must first define what living really means.

In a society where the tapestry of our lives is often woven with threads of sacrifice for others, the pursuit of personal grace becomes a revolutionary act. As women, we are nurtured in environments that exalt the virtue of self-sacrifice—rising before dawn, tirelessly toiling, maintaining the hearth, and nurturing those around us. This deeply ingrained model, instilled from childhood, often seeds silent resentments, feelings that simmer among women who congregate to vent about the relentless demands of life. This sanctuary, affectionately dubbed the "hen house" in my family, morphs into a fleeting refuge that provides nothing but more seeds of resentment.

Financially, the script we're handed is riddled with contradictions. We earn less yet shoulder more expectations. If we dare to prioritize our own needs, the label of selfishness is pasted on and fixed. It's a pervasive lose-lose scenario, ensnaring countless women in a web of financial and emotional disempowerment.

For women to ascend as financial leaders and visionaries on a global scale, we must undertake a profound inward journey.

This journey involves the dismantling of antiquated financial paradigms and the forging of new ones that venerate our deepest selves and values. It transcends the mere tactics of saving more or spending less; it's about fundamentally redefining our relationships with money in a way that transforms our lives and the world around us.

Embarking on a transformative journey with your finances isn't just a matter of adjusting your budget—it's about fundamentally reshaping your life's narrative. This journey requires unwavering clarity of vision and firm nonnegotiables. These are not merely practical financial terms, but rather beacons that illuminate your path through the dense fog of life's myriad decisions.

To begin, you must engage in a process of deep self-reflection to uncover what you truly desire. This step is about more than identifying your material or financial wants; it involves connecting with your core values and what you seek to achieve in life. Whether it's freeing yourself from the shackles of debt, owning your home outright, or pursuing further education, each goal must resonate deeply with your personal aspirations and ethics. These goals become the lighthouses that guide your decisions, helping you navigate through the complexities of life without losing sight of your destination.

Just as crucial is defining your nonnegotiables—those conditions or standards you are not willing to compromise on. This might include not incurring additional debt, setting a boundary against risky financial ventures (or vice versa—taking risk!), or dedicating a portion of your income to savings no matter the circumstances. These nonnegotiables act as guardrails, keeping you aligned with your financial and personal integrity as you move forward.

Next, you've got to take a look in the mirror. This means taking a hard, unflinching look at your current financial situation and behaviors. Are there patterns of money coming and money going out that conflict with your stated goals? Are you holding onto habits or beliefs about money that stem from fear rather than fact? This level of honesty can be uncomfortable, as it forces you to confront aspects of your financial life that you may have been avoiding or denying.

Once you've established a clear vision and recognized your current standing, the next step is to take new and uncharted actions with your finances. This could mean restructuring your budget in ways that feel unfamiliar, investing in areas you've previously avoided due to uncertainty, or even changing your career path to better align with your financial goals. These actions require not just courage, but a willingness to step into the unknown, trusting that these choices will lead you to a more secure and fulfilling financial future.

To truly transform, you must be willing to let your old financial self go, as if shedding a cocoon to birth a new identity. This metamorphic process involves releasing outdated habits, beliefs, and identities that no longer nurture your growth. It's like stepping into a new world where each decision and action is a deliberate push into the light of your fully realized potential, aligned with the life you are destined to create.

As you divorce your old patterns and embrace new practices, you give birth to a new financial identity. This rebirth is not a sudden transformation but a gradual process of becoming more attuned to your financial environment and more responsive to changes and opportunities. As you grow into this new identity, you will find that your previously unattainable goals begin to seem within reach, and your financial decisions become more proactive rather than reactive.

Vision and clarity in your financial life are about much more than knowing your bank account balance or keeping a budget. They involve a holistic understanding of your financial narrative, a commitment to reshaping that narrative, and the courage to act boldly in pursuit of your dreams. By being brutally honest with yourself and daring to take uncharted actions, you set the stage for a profound personal and financial transformation. Remember, each step forward in this journey not only brings you closer to your financial goals but also to becoming the person you aspire to be.

This path is not an easy path. It is one that is often met with resistance and turbulence and it is exactly what it will take for women on our planet to unanimously thrive.

True financial planning is not about conforming to societal molds; it's about sculpting a life that resonates with the essence of who you are. This may mean adopting some conventional financial strategies, but more often than not, you'll need to blaze a trail that is distinctly yours, peppered with customized strategies that mirror your personal values and lifestyle.

Living a life aligned with your true self is the bedrock of sustainable financial health. Deciding what you genuinely want and what you are willing to strive for lays the foundation for true fulfillment and financial success. It is imperative to steer clear of the deafening allure of passing trends and concentrate on what genuinely matters to you.

To sum it up, fall in love with yourself. Fall deeply and madly in love with who you are, and say no to anything that threatens to take you off your path. Be genuine and be confident that as you fall in love with yourself, you will also find deeper purpose and satisfaction in this world. There is no one who will not benefit from his journey because a person who loves themselves deeply has the ability to love others just as deeply. This is a formula for success across the planet.

This is the journey of healing.

BIG-PICTURE THINKING AND BAD-BITCH ENERGY

Remember Clara? She started her journey with baby steps, slowly healing her relationship with money. It wasn't easy—she had to pick off the scabs, confront her financial narrative, and have the courage to say what she really wanted out of life. But with a little lip gloss, a strong coffee, and some much-needed support, she reminded herself just how powerful she is.

Clara didn't just settle for surviving; she embraced her big-picture vision. She realized that taking radical responsibility for her life wasn't just about her bank account—it was about every aspect of her life, from her career to her well-being. With each small step, she aligned her daily actions with her long-term goals, all while staying grounded with breathwork, yoga, and NLP visualization.

And when things got tough, she didn't hesitate to call in her support system. Whether it was a friend, coach, or simply her own inner voice reminding her of her worth, she knew she didn't have to go it alone.

We all have a little Clara inside us. With a bit of support, some lip gloss, and a strong cup of coffee, we can tackle anything life throws our way.

Let's keep our eyes on the big picture and never forget: We're bad bitches who can do anything.

JOURNALING PROMPTS

Stop Budgeting, Start Living
The Time to Heal Is Here and Now

1. Defining What Living Means to You

    How do you define "living" in your own life? What does a life truly lived look and feel like for you? How does this definition align with your current reality, and where do you see room for growth?

2. Exploring the Burden of Sacrifice

    Reflect on the sacrifices you've made for others in your life. How have these sacrifices shaped your identity and your financial situation? Are there areas where you've compromised too much of yourself, and what would it look like to reclaim those parts?

3. Uncovering Silent Resentments

    Think about the areas in your life where you may feel unacknowledged or taken for granted. How have these feelings of resentment impacted your relationship with money and your sense of self-worth? What steps can you take to address and heal these resentments?

4. Identifying Your Vision and Nonnegotiables

    What is your vision for your life, financially and otherwise? What are the nonnegotiables—values, goals, or boundaries—that you are unwilling to compromise on as you work toward this vision? How can you ensure these guide your decisions moving forward?

5. Confronting Your Financial Reality

   Take a hard, honest look at your current financial situation. Are there patterns or behaviors that conflict with your goals? What fears or beliefs have been holding you back, and how can you begin to address them?

6. Taking Uncharted Actions

   What new, bold actions can you take to align your financial life with your vision? What old habits or beliefs need to be left behind as you move forward? How can you embrace the discomfort that comes with stepping into the unknown?

7. Divorcing Your Old Financial Self

   What aspects of your past financial identity no longer serve you? How can you symbolically divorce yourself from these outdated beliefs and behaviors? What new financial identity are you ready to embrace?

8. Building a New Financial Identity

   As you create a new relationship with money, what values and practices will be at the core of your financial life? How will this new identity empower you to achieve your goals and live more authentically?

9. Healing Through Self-Love

   How can you deepen your love and acceptance of yourself as you navigate this journey of financial and personal transformation? In what ways can self-love fuel your financial success and overall well-being?

10. Big-Picture Thinking and Resilience

    Reflect on your long-term goals and the big-picture vision for your life. How can you stay focused on this vision even when faced with challenges? What support systems do you have or need to cultivate to help you stay resilient and empowered on your journey?

PART FIVE
CONSCIOUS REDESIGN

THE STOP BUDGETING PLAYBOOK

If you want a stronger house, you must build a stronger foundation.

Have you ever felt torn between enjoying your money now and being responsible for saving later? You're so not alone. This is a conversation that I have on a daily basis with clients who feel torn between wanting to enjoy your money today and making sure they have enough for tomorrow and for the long haul. As women with money, we've been conditioned to say no, cut back, and feel guilty for spending money. We've been told that it shouldn't feel good to say yes to spending; even just saying that makes me feel sick to my stomach.

It's time to change the money conversation around spending. And I'm so glad you're here, because in this section of the book, I'm sharing some practical tips on:

- How you can say yes more
- Why you want to when it comes to money
- How you can eliminate guilt and shame that come with spending

- How you can expand your financial emotional intelligence by embracing a healthy relationship with spending

All right, so I've been in the finance industry for the last ten years, and traditional finance often focuses on saying no to spending. We've been listening for years to financial experts who have been telling us that we have to cut back and stop spending, and that that's the root of all of our financial pain. But what if I told you that it's this sacrificial approach to money management that has created so much shame and fear when it comes to money? How do I know this? I work with clients daily who tell me that they're beating themselves up for the choices they're making financially, and it's just time for a new approach.

What would it feel like to not regret a decision that you've made financially, immediately or the next week? As one of my clients put it, last week, she immediately regretted buying a hat that she knew she would never wear. So why did she do it? Our purchasing decisions happen in the unconscious mind, and after processing through this event with her, she realized that she bought the hat because she wanted to be liked. It was actually her fear of rejection that had her buy the hat. She wanted to be liked by the store owner. That was the reason she bought the hat. What she learned from this, having talked through what was going on in her unconscious mind as she made the purchase, she also learned that she doesn't need to buy anything from anyone to have them like her. This is so powerful because she was able to identify the root cause of the decision to buy the hat, and she felt really guilty after buying the hat.

Well, the finance industry isn't doing a great job of helping us relieve that shame and guilt and get to the root cause of the decisions that we're making. For this client, she realizes that in the future, she can draw from this learning and work to eliminate her buyer's remorse forever.

Does this sound like something that you can relate to? If you really want to change the way that you're spending money so that you can feel good about the decisions that you're making, you've got to get to work immediately to understand the reasons behind the decisions that you are making. The finance industry has done a terrible job of making you feel like you're stupid or impulsive when it comes to spending right here, right now.

We're going to shift this conversation into something much more powerful and approachable, and we're going to reframe your relationship with spending forever. Instead of saying no to the things you want because you don't think you can afford them, or because spending is bad, I want you to learn how to say yes to the things that you really do want. Yes is way more powerful and leads to long-term financial well-being. So how do we start to change that? One of my clients landed a $5,000 deal. It was a big client that she landed, and she texted me immediately. My response to her was, "Amazing, congratulations, good job."

And then I told her to go spend $500 on herself. She called that a butt-pucker moment. It made her stretch outside of her comfort zone, because in her head, she was supposed to hold on to all of that money. Save it for a rainy day. And whether it's a client deal that you've made or a bonus that you've made for work, some of your dis-ease and not necessarily your own fault necessarily: You've been taught that you should hold on to that, and that's a very scarcity mindset. By just giving herself $500, 10 percent of what she made, she gave herself permission to enjoy something that she could really love. That's a way of shifting the framework and the context of spending altogether. The rest of it, put away, use for your business, whatever it is that you need it for. Put some in savings. All good. But what if you could just enjoy it a little bit more? What would be possible for you?

Another example of this is I have a client who is going to be inheriting over $800,000. These questions come to me all the time about inheritances. What should I do with it? Well, the finance industry would say be responsible, right? Be responsible. Pay off debt, put it in savings, tuck it away as if it never existed at all. I agree with some of that, but I also told this client to take 5 percent of that and go enjoy it. Just cut off a little bit of that. Do something for yourself. Take yourself to a spa day, give yourself gratitude and grace for this windfall, and then put a game plan together for the rest of it. I'm going to give you some tips today in this chapter about how you can start saying more yes and less no financially, and there's a huge payoff for you to have the ability to spend now, enjoy now, and know that you're taking care of your financial future. So let's get started. Tip number one: Start saying yes to spending.

You've got to flip the script on yourself. Wouldn't it be amazing to walk into a store, take a stroll downtown, pass through a farmers' market, and be able to say yes with confidence that you can afford what you're choosing to buy, and you know exactly why you're saying yes? This requires you to have a much healthier and more intentional relationship with your money.

Most of us are operating out of our pasts and out of our unconscious minds. When we clean that up, we can start making choices with intention and purpose. Tip number two: Decide on what you want to say yes to. Saying yes to what you want is what you must do immediately if you're going to reduce guilt, shame, and stress around spending. Cookie-cutter approaches to money mean that someone else is telling you what's important for you to spend your money on. And I think that's bullshit.

It's time for you to get in a conscious, active relationship with your money and give yourself permission to say yes to more things that bring you joy in your life. You did not come into this life to live someone else's life. Get to know yourself at your deepest values. Ask what's important to you. There's no wrong answer. This is going to help you say yes to more more often, and that's how you start to heal your relationship with money. Tip number three: Balance present enjoyment with future goals. One of the most common challenges to saying yes is that you don't actually know what you have to spend versus what you save. So many people come to me because they feel disorganized and like their financial life is chaos.

So when you get that under control, you can really start to separate out what you have to spend versus what you need to save. It can all feel very overwhelming if you're all looking at it together. So you've got to get organized first. It does not mean budgeting. You can absolutely have what you want in your life without budgeting. What I want you to hear is that you can enjoy your money now and be responsible. It's not either/or; responsibility means meeting your needs and wants and still being able to plan for your future. Here are a few strategies to learn how to balance it all. First, get a clear picture of what money you have coming in and money that you have going out. Do a thirty-day audit, and look specifically at your spending money. What did you spend your money on? This is not meant to drive you down the wormhole of shame and guilt, but it comes from a place of awareness. If you know where your money's going, then you can make some new decisions with where you want it to go in the future. After doing your audit, you can realign your spending into categories.

I invite you to do that audit, and then look at what you spent your money on. Look back and say, "Okay, of the things that I spent money on, what here is negotiable? What can I live without? What is just spending that I don't need?" And then look at one of those things that are nonnegotiable. I would say that food is nonnegotiable. How much you spend on food is negotiable, but the fact that you're going to feed your family is not negotiable. So be realistic about it, but look at your spending and ask yourself, "What's negotiable? What's not negotiable?"

That's a really healthy exercise for you to start to get an idea of how much money you need to spend versus what you are spending, maybe out of the unconscious mind, because it's just been programmed into you to do it. Get clear and present regarding what you're spending, right here, right now. The easiest thing to do to get control of your spending right here, right now, is to set up a spending account. Once you understand what you're spending your money on, every single week, put money into a spending account. This doesn't require you to budget.

You don't have to get into the nitty gritty of where every penny goes. Two of my clients just did this in the last week, and they've each already paid off one credit card just by putting money into a spending account.

It's a lifesaver, and it'll help you get clearer and more organized with the money that you're spending. It's going to help you spend with more joy. Another thing that you can do to set it and forget it, so that you know that you have money going to long-term savings is automate your savings every single paycheck. Designate a fixed amount, fifty to a hundred dollars, to go to savings. I would recommend the savings account is actually not a part of your everyday checking account. Open it up at another bank and send it over there.

Set up savings and forget about it.

Altogether, you can start to rewire your relationship with money by having money to spend and saying yes to the things that bring you joy. That's going to help you live your most authentic life. Tuck money aside, set it and forget it. We do this in my household. It's amazing, and these few steps are going to help you create a healthier, happier relationship with money. No budgets required.

SMOKE AND MIRRORS

It's all smoke and mirrors. Budgets. We have been told that if we don't budget, we suck. And, if we can't budget, we're stupid or have impulse control problems. We've been told that the only way to be successful is to sacrifice, and that all we have to do is just work a little harder.

It's all bullshit.

Life will not magically fall into place with a budget. So, fuck it. Toss it out. Forget about it. You do not need a budget.

Most people create a budget out of guilt that they don't have one (after all, we're told that all responsible adults should), but they don't *actually* want to use it. It's annoying and restrictive, and it just ends up in a drawer next to a stack of user guides and decks of playing cards wrapped in plastic.

If you hate the word "budget" as much as I do, I'm giving you permission to stop budgeting forever.

My client Laura completely transformed her life by shifting her mindset. Growing up in poverty, she had always been driven by a scarcity mentality. Despite running a successful multi-million-dollar business with her husband, James, she couldn't understand why they were still in debt. James believed a strict budget was the ultimate solution—after all, that's what they'd always been told was the key to fixing money problems—but it wasn't clicking for her. On top of that, Laura felt so behind financially that she didn't think they deserved to spend money on "frivolous" things or enjoy life.

I challenged her to rethink this. "What if you set aside money specifically for fun?" Her immediate response was, "Hell yeah—I can do that!" That simple shift changed everything. Laura and her family of five just returned from a nine-day trip to Italy, creating memories they'll cherish forever. When you stop using a budget as an excuse for why you can't live the life you want, you open the door to dreaming—and achieving—again.

BUDGETS WORKED FOR OUR GRANDPARENTS...NOT US

Budgets *did* work for a very specific set of people. Back in the Depression era, most Americans had very small amounts of cash, no credit cards, and no viable way to take on debt. If they wanted to purchase something, they had to have the money with which to do so. Even if they might not have used the specific terminology, something resembling a budget would have been useful in ensuring they had enough cash for upcoming purchases throughout the remainder of the month.

However, society has changed completely since this time. For one thing, women now hold jobs and many households are dual income. Additionally, most people rarely (if ever) use cash anymore. There is also no longer a fixed mindset about staying at the same job for one's whole life: Doing so probably wouldn't even occur to most millennials and Gen Z people.

Unfortunately, financial advice has largely *not* evolved accordingly. We still cling to budgets as the gold standard in money management, but they were created for a part of the population that no longer exists or is dying out quickly. We need something more flexible for today's lifestyles.

I see it time and time again with my clients: People come to me with a real fear-based mentality around their own money. They don't trust that it is working effectively for them, and they don't trust that they know how to handle it on their own. I understand how money management can be overwhelming, especially if you feel like you're starting from ten steps behind where you perceive other people to be. But ladies, come on! It's *our* money. We have to learn how to manage it correctly to make sure it's working as hard as possible for us.

YOUR NEW BFF: THE THREE-ACCOUNT SYSTEM

Most clients that come to me are doing all their banking and spending out of a single account. They can open up their banking app, but still have no idea what is going on because everything is commingled. This also makes it very difficult to bounce back if they overspend in a particular category. Using only one account really doesn't make sense, because there's not just one reason we have money. In fact, there are three. One is to operate our households. Another is to save (not hoard—just save!). The third is to enjoy our lives.

As an example of what it looks like to have accounts for different purposes, my husband and I put $600 in our household spending account every single week. All I need to know is that between Wednesday and Wednesday, I have $600 for groceries, entertainment, eating out, or whatever I want. Importantly (and unlike a budget), I am *not* tracking the allocation of how that money is being spent. The only thing I need to focus on is how much is left. Maybe on Tuesday afternoon I decide that I want to buy a new shirt. I look in the account and see that we have twenty-nine dollars left, but the shirt costs more than that. No problem—I'll just wait until the next day when another $600 gets deposited into the account. We then have other accounts for savings and life enjoyment activities (like vacations). Rather than restrict our spending and keep us in a scarcity mentality, this system gives us *permission* to spend.

The truth is that most people have spent the majority of their lives feeling ashamed of their financial choices, embarrassed that they have debt, and nervous that they don't have enough saved for retirement. Once you give yourself permission to spend the money that is ours without judgment or guilt, it breaks you out of the paycheck-to-paycheck cycle and helps you take charge to build your life the way you want.

WHAT THE NUMBERS ARE ACTUALLY COMMUNICATING

Regardless of how much money they make, most Americans are living paycheck to paycheck (yes, even those with salaries in the six figures). Here's the thing, though—*we all have money*. We're just often not being very intentional or informed about where it is going.

A financial inventory is a key piece of my process for understanding what my clients spend and keep in a month. It's wildly easy. Total up the household's paychecks from the past three months (in case there were any fluctuations). That tells you how much money came in on average. Then look at how much money flowed out over the past three months. This is not the step where we're changing behavior at all; it's only about building awareness about our patterns. If I had to guess, I'd bet you will realize that you have a lot more money to spend than you think you do. This is what happens for most of my clients.

For example, my client Alison and her husband are in their twenties and live in Florida with their two young kids. In their minds, they were living paycheck to paycheck. Money was a common source of tension, and they felt like they were constantly playing tug-of-war with each other around their spending habits. We did an inventory of their ninety days, and they realized that they actually had $3,500 to spend after paying bills. Seeing their money in a new way, and armed with that knowledge, they were able to decide for themselves how to separate money based on purpose and identify what was negotiable or nonnegotiable.

Another client couple in their forties made a similar discovery. He's a police officer, she is a nurse, and they felt like they were completely broke. When they did their financial inventory and tracked their net worth for the first time, they realized that they were actually millionaires. They also had $4,000 to spend after bills every month. It was such a wake-up call for them. If you're reading this, it's likely you do have money. Maybe you don't feel like you do, and that's the emotional relationship with money that needs to be addressed. To start from the frontlines of your financial life—you just need to be clear about where it is and where it's going.

THE MAGIC: SEPARATE ACCOUNTS

After you finish our financial inventory, it's time for the exciting part: deciding how much money is going to go into our three different accounts (operating, saving, and fun). Let's imagine that you go through the inventory exercise and discover that you have $2,000 to spend every month. That means you have

$500 to spend each week. I recommend sticking with this weekly allocation rather than monthly, because it's more aligned with the regular rhythm of life. We might get paid biweekly or even monthly, but we tend to envision our schedules on a week-to-week basis. It's easier to think, "Okay, I have $500 to spend each week and I only need to make it until next Wednesday with that money" rather than "Well, I have to somehow make this $2,000 last all month."

Once you know your total weekly allowance, the choice is yours about how to divide it between accounts. You might decide to put $300 per week in your operating account, one hundred dollars in savings, and one hundred dollars in fun. Or maybe you're saving for a big vacation and decide to allocate a higher percentage to fun and cut back on your operating expenses. Everyone has different needs; we're not trying to put you in a box.

The organization of the three-account system is also in our hands. I generally advise clients to set up three separate accounts, but you also need to do it in accordance with whatever works best for our life. For example, one of the women I work with banks at Chase but has her spending account set up through Ally. She likes having a bit more separation, and that it's out of sight and out of mind. Regardless of how you set it up, the three-account system gets you out of the paycheck-to-paycheck cycle because it takes the guesswork out of our finances and gives you a framework for how to spend our money.

FREEDOM = GUILT-FREE SPENDING

There's this dichotomy in our society where we're constantly being marketed to *(Spend more money! Buy the Louis Vuitton handbag and everyone will admire you!)* while simultaneously being mocked for our spending choices. Financial experts are often instigators of this: If you go on their pages, they are constantly converting designer purchases into retirement savings or belittling people for buying expensive lattes rather than making their own at home. This tug-of-war creates unease around spending and causes people to feel guilty about their purchases.

This is the beauty of our shiny new spending account. Its entire purpose is for you to spend the money in it. After all, you have another account for saving: You're not stealing from that balance by spending this one. Instead, you're creating permission around your decisions and giving yourself the authority to use your money as you want. Involved with this is identifying your why around your choices. When you buy something, what is its purpose in life? How does it serve your vision or goals for your life? If you can lock in on those answers, you start to look forward to spending money intentionally rather than emotionally.

When I met my client Jennie, she was living in New York and working in sales for a high-end clothing brand. Jennie had gotten into a habit of spending money, particularly to enhance her wardrobe, because she felt like she had to keep up with her friends and coworkers. When we put the three-account system in place, her overspending stopped almost immediately. She was finally able to look at her closet and think, "I have enough. I actually have *more* than enough."

Once she changed how she thought about money, Jennie realized that she was worth much more than she was getting paid at work. I coached her to start advocating for herself in her team, and Jennie was ultimately able to double her salary in just under a year of working with me.

Through tracking her money and finally understanding her own value, Jennie has been able to pay off credit cards and travel the world with zero guilt. Like Jennie, most people's pain point with money has to do with spending. When we are able to shift our mentality around spending, it transforms our entire relationship with money.

THE SECRET TO SAVING

If you listen to some financial experts, they'll tell you that you should have six to twelve months of expenses saved up for emergencies. But how attainable does that feel if you're one of the 75 percent of Americans living paycheck to paycheck? Probably not very. Instead, let's take a more realistic approach to our savings goals using the three-account system.

We need to first make sure you're saving for the things you're already spending money on. For example, what happens when you have it drilled into your head that you must have money in an account for emergencies, but then want to take a vacation? You either pull from your emergency fund (and feel guilty about it), or put the vacation expenses on a credit card (and feel guilty about it). Both paths create shame around a decision that should have been exciting. I've had clients come into my office in tears because they're burned out and don't see a path for being able to go on vacation with their families. This is not what life is about, friends.

Ultimately, we want to think about saving in two ways: an allocation for fun and experiences (like vacations), and another for the inevitable expenses that arise in life (like new tires for the car). These are the items that can often feel like emergencies if you're unprepared, but can instead feel like mild inconveniences when you are.

Once you become a pro at the three-account system, there is flexibility to open additional accounts and get really granular with how you are allocating your money. Perhaps you eventually have subaccounts for savings, where you keep vacation money, house down payment funds, and car repair money all separate.

Don't worry about that quite yet, but understand that the power ultimately always resides in our hands to save for the things that will enhance our lives.

INVESTING TRIFECTA

When most people think of investing, the first thing that comes to mind is common financial vehicles like stocks and real estate.

There are actually three ways to invest: time, people, and money.

They're all related to one another. If you're not happy with the financial results you're getting in your life, it's time to look inward and examine your relationships and how you are spending your time. I sometimes don't even talk numbers with new clients until our second or third meeting; our conversation centers instead on getting them to look inward.

People often use money to stuff down their feelings or cover the things that are going on in their lives. I've worked with clients who don't have a solid routine in the morning and always feel like they're behind schedule. They rush out the door in a cloud of stress and stop by the coffee shop on the ground floor of their office to pick up a bagel and a shot of espresso. One of my clients was spending twenty-five dollars on coffee and breakfast every single day simply because she wasn't giving herself enough time in the morning to get ready.

There is absolutely nothing wrong with that if it's genuinely intentional or something that brings her fulfillment. It's all about lifestyle and preference versus scarcity, fear, and survival.

One of my other clients came to me $100,000 in debt because she didn't have solid boundaries with a toxic man in her life. *That's not a money problem; it's a people problem.* Her emotional bank account was out of whack. Once she addressed the way she was being treated, her finances flowed from there. A budget is not going to have this conversation with you. You need to be able to have a loving conversation with yourself and do an audit of the people in your life.

There are two things to do to get started with this audit. The first is to examine how you are spending our time. Get out an Excel spreadsheet or a clean piece of paper and track your movement over a two-week period. This will lead you to how you are spending our money. Second, make a list of the top ten people you spend time with regularly. Consider each one from a deposit or withdrawal perspective.

Are they constantly making emotional demands from you but never depositing anything positive? Being aware of who potentially falls on that spectrum allows you to cut them from our life or just be more aware of the influence they might have. Ultimately, you'll start surrounding yourself with people who celebrate your choices and inspire you to continue making them.

FINANCIAL FORECASTING

Why This Is a Game Changer for My Clients

Taking control of your finances can often feel overwhelming, especially when the future seems uncertain. Many of us have experienced that gut-wrenching anxiety that wakes us up in the middle of the night, drenched in cold sweat, worrying about money. I know this feeling all too well—even though managing finances is what I do for a living. That's why I developed a practical, hands-on approach that not only helps alleviate that anxiety, but also empowers my clients to take control of their financial futures.

One of the most powerful tools I've created for my clients is my twelve-month financial tracker. This simple yet effective Excel sheet allows clients to input their current financial data—income, expenses, investments, and savings—and see how these numbers will evolve over the next year. By laying everything out in black and red, clients can easily visualize how their financial decisions today will impact their goals tomorrow.

What Works About It

The twelve-month financial tracker is designed to be user-friendly, even for those who may not feel confident with numbers or spreadsheets.

Here's what I teach my clients to do in my Stop Budgeting Course:

1. *Input Your Data*: Start by entering your current financial information—your income, fixed expenses, discretionary spending, savings, and investments. The tracker is flexible enough to accommodate different types of

income and expenses, making it suitable for various financial situations.
2. *Forecast Your Financial Future*: Once your data is entered, the tracker automatically calculates and projects your financial situation month by month. It takes into account factors like recurring expenses, irregular income, and planned investments or savings contributions.
3. *Visualize the Impact of Your Choices*: The beauty of this tool is in its visual representation. You can see at a glance how your net worth will change over time based on your current financial habits. The tracker highlights areas where you may need to cut back or where you have room to invest more. This clear, objective view helps remove the guesswork and provides you with a roadmap to financial stability.
4. *Make Adjustments in Real Time*: Life is unpredictable, and so is money. The tracker allows you to update your information as your situation changes, whether that's a pay raise, an unexpected expense, or a new financial goal. By regularly revisiting and updating the tracker, you stay proactive in managing your finances, rather than reacting to unexpected surprises.

THE JOURNEY TO FINANCIAL EMPOWERMENT

Taking charge of your money isn't just about managing today's bills—it's about building a future where you feel secure and empowered. The twelve-month financial tracker is a foundational tool in this journey. It helps you create a clear financial picture, anticipate potential challenges, and make informed decisions that align with your long-term goals.

As you continue to use the tracker, you'll notice how your financial awareness and confidence grow. You'll start to think ahead, planning not just for the next month, but for the years to come. This proactive approach is a game changer because it shifts your mindset from one of fear and uncertainty to one of control and empowerment. You're no longer just reacting to financial stress; you're actively shaping your financial future.

By integrating this tracker into your routine, you take the first step toward financial mastery. It's a journey, not a destination, but with each step, you're building a stronger foundation for the life you want. And as your life evolves, so too will your financial systems, allowing you to stay aligned with your goals and aspirations.

Homework and Next Steps

1. **Reflect on your current relationship with money.** Think about your feelings toward money and spending. Recall a recent purchase that made you feel guilty or anxious. What emotions or beliefs drove that decision? Consider how you can shift your mindset to make future purchases that align with your values and bring you joy without guilt.
2. **Conduct a thirty-day financial audit.** Track every dollar you spend for the next thirty days without judging or restricting yourself. Simply observe where your money is going. At the end of the thirty days, categorize your spending into negotiable and nonnegotiable items. This will give you a clear picture of your financial habits and help you make intentional changes.
3. **Implement the three-account system.** Set up three separate accounts: one for operating expenses, one for

savings, and one for fun or enjoyment. Allocate your income across these accounts based on your financial audit results. Start using these accounts to manage your money intentionally and guilt free.

4. **Start saying yes to spending.** Identify one area of your life where you've been saying no to spending out of fear or guilt. This week, flip the script and say yes. Whether it's treating yourself to something small or investing in an experience, allow yourself to enjoy spending without the usual anxiety.

5. **Develop a savings habit.** Automate your savings by setting up a direct deposit or automatic transfer to your savings account each time you get paid. Start with an amount that feels comfortable, and increase it as your financial situation improves. The goal is to build a habit of saving, not to stress over the amount.

6. **Conduct a financial inventory.** Take stock of your financial situation over the past three months by calculating your total income, expenses, and savings. This exercise will help you understand where your money is going and how you can better align it with your goals.

7. **Use a twelve-month financial tracker.** Begin using a twelve-month financial tracker to project your finances over the next year. Input your current financial data and regularly update it to reflect changes in your income, expenses, and goals. Use this tracker to visualize your progress and adjust your financial strategies in real time.

8. **Define your nonnegotiables.** Write down your financial and personal nonnegotiables—those things you refuse to compromise on. These could include setting boundaries with debt, committing to savings, or prioritizing

self-care through spending. Keep this list visible to guide your financial decisions.
9. **Reevaluate your financial goals.** After conducting your financial audit and inventory, reassess your financial goals. Are they still aligned with your values and current situation? Adjust them as necessary to ensure they reflect what you truly want out of life.
10. **Celebrate your wins.** Set aside time each week to review your financial progress and celebrate your wins, no matter how small. This practice reinforces positive behaviors and helps you stay motivated on your journey to financial empowerment.

By diving into these steps, you're setting yourself up for a stronger, more intentional relationship with money. This isn't about restrictive budgeting; it's about embracing a financial future that's empowering, fulfilling, and filled with joy. I know you want that, and it's time for you to have it!

THE END IS
THE BEGINNING

A JOURNEY TO WHOLENESS

As I sit here, reflecting on the journey that brought me to this moment, I'm reminded of a truth that's as powerful as it is undeniable: The most profound transformations in life often stem from the hardest decisions we ever have to make. My divorce was one of those decisions. It wasn't just the end of a marriage; it was the beginning of a new life—one that required me to risk everything I had known to discover the woman I was truly meant to be.

Ending my marriage was terrifying. It felt like stepping into the unknown, leaving behind the safety net of the familiar. I had to confront the possibility of losing my sense of stability, my identity as a wife, and the life I had painstakingly built over many years. But deep down, I knew that staying would mean losing something far more precious—myself. It was a choice between continuing a life that no longer felt true or risking it all to find out who I really was and what I was capable of becoming.

The path wasn't easy. There were days when I questioned everything—when the fear of the unknown nearly paralyzed me. But each step forward, no matter how small, brought me closer to the woman I was meant to become. I had to let go of the life I thought I was supposed to live to embrace the life that was waiting for me.

And let me tell you, it has been so, so worth it.

Through this journey, I've learned that the end is never truly the end; it's just the beginning of something new. When I look back at the woman I was before, I see someone who was afraid to let go, afraid to step into the unknown. But by doing so, I found my true self.

If I could sit down with my younger self, the first thing I'd tell her is to say no more often. Say no to anything that doesn't make you feel truly alive—like take-your-breath-away alive. Say no to anything that isn't a burning desire. And, for the love of everything sacred, slow down. Slow the fuck down. Watch the birds sing. Hold hands just a little longer. Sleep in. Walk often. Pay attention to the things that bring you closer to God—like the way the waves pull in and out, the way nature reminds us that life is a series of ebbs and flows.

The little girl I used to be is still in there, deep inside. She's adventurous, determined, funny, mischievous, a risk-taker, loving, quiet, smart, inquisitive, hungry for knowledge, compassionate, and curious. I think those qualities scared the hell out of my dad. I didn't get love for being that way, so I buried those parts of myself. I buried them in work, in alcohol, in fame, in achievements, in debt. And in writing this, I can feel myself healing those parts of me.

I lost sight of who I was because I was too busy trying to be who I thought I needed to be. But in writing this book, I've given myself permission to be me again. And in doing so, I've realized just how many women around the world are still trapped, unable to embrace their true selves because of the roles they feel forced to play.

I'm giving myself permission to be myself. This book is a reminder to you, and to myself, that we are whole. We are beautiful, and we are enough just as we are. We don't need to chase after external validation or bury ourselves in things that don't serve us. What we really want is simple—connection, love, and to know that we matter. These, not the complicated stories we often tell ourselves, are the things that truly fulfill us.

And here's what I want to share with you now: You have the power to create the life you desire and to inspire others to join you in that journey. Start now, and watch how the world around you begins to transform. Right here, and right now, have the courage to trust that you are enough as you are, and that your value isn't tied to how perfectly you can orchestrate your life. The real strength lies in facing that fear, letting go of the need to control, and allowing yourself to experience life in all its messy, unpredictable glory. This is where true growth happens. This is where you find the courage to live a life that's richer, more meaningful, and authentically yours.

As I conclude this book, I'm reminded that the end is never really the end. It's the beginning of something new, something beautiful. It's the start of living a life that is true to who you are, without apology or hesitation. So, to you, I say this: Embrace the endings in your life, because they are the gateways to new beginnings. Trust that you are whole, you are beautiful, and you are enough. The world is waiting for you to step into your power, to live authentically, and to create the life you've always dreamed of.

And for the love of God, stop budgeting.

XO,
Lisa

APPENDIX: GLOSSARY OF TERMS

Radical responsibility: The concept of taking complete ownership of your actions, decisions, and outcomes in life. It's about acknowledging that you have the power to shape your life, particularly in your financial choices, and not blaming external circumstances or others for your situation.

Financial set point: Unconscious financial thresholds or limits that are influenced by upbringing, beliefs, and past experiences. This individual set point often determines how much financial success or struggle we feel comfortable with.

Money personality: The specific behaviors, attitudes, and beliefs about money that shape how you manage your finances. Your money personality is often formed by childhood experiences and can influence your financial decisions as an adult.

Neuro-linguistic programming (NLP): A psychological approach that involves analyzing strategies used by successful individuals and applying them to reach personal goals. It's used to understand and change thought patterns and behaviors.

Forgiveness: In the context of financial healing, it's the process of letting go of guilt, shame, and negative self-judgment related to past financial decisions.

Resilience: The ability to recover from setbacks and continue moving forward. In finance, it's about learning from mistakes and adapting to challenges without losing sight of your goals.

Emotional bank account: A metaphor for the level of trust, respect, and goodwill in a relationship. Just like a financial bank account, there are deposits (positive actions) and withdrawals (negative actions).

Toxic relationships: Relationships that drain your emotional and financial resources. These relationships often involve one party consistently failing to meet their commitments, leading to a negative impact on the other party's emotional and financial well-being.

Boundaries: Limits that you set in relationships to protect your emotional and financial well-being. Healthy boundaries ensure that your needs are met without compromising your values or financial security.

Underearning: The habit or pattern of consistently earning less than your potential or worth. This is often influenced by limiting beliefs, financial set points, and societal expectations.

Financial inventory: A comprehensive review of your income, expenses, assets, and liabilities over a specific period. It helps to create awareness of your financial habits and patterns.

Scarcity mindset: A belief that resources, including money, are limited, leading to fear, anxiety, and a tendency to hoard wealth or avoid spending. This mindset contrasts with an abundance mindset, which focuses on the availability of resources.

Radical honesty: Being completely truthful with yourself about your desires, goals, and current situation, even when it's uncomfortable. It's the foundation for making meaningful changes in your life.

Willingness: The readiness to confront your fears, face the truth, and take the necessary steps to create change. It's a key component of personal and financial growth.

Trust in action: Demonstrating your belief in yourself and your financial goals through consistent, intentional actions. It involves aligning your behaviors with your values and the outcomes you want to achieve.

TRUST framework: A five-pillar approach to building a healthy relationship with money, consisting of Tracking, Return on Investment (ROI), Understanding Your Why, Systems, and Tools.

Tracking: Monitoring your income and expenses to gain clarity on your financial situation. It's the first step in taking control of your finances.

Return on investment (ROI): The value or benefit derived from a particular financial decision or purchase. It's about assessing whether your spending aligns with your values and contributes positively to your life.

Systems: Organized methods or processes that help manage your finances efficiently. Systems can include bank account structures, savings plans, or budgeting tools.

Tools: Resources, such as apps or financial trackers, that assist in managing your money more effectively.

Shadow work: The process of exploring the unconscious parts of yourself, particularly those aspects that you may deny or suppress, such as fears, doubts, and insecurities. Shadow work is essential for personal growth and healing.

Root chakra: In energy healing, the root chakra is associated with feelings of safety, security, and financial stability. An imbalance in this chakra can manifest as financial insecurity or unhealthy financial behaviors.

Energy work: A holistic approach to healing that involves balancing the body's energy systems, often through practices like Reiki or chakra work. It's used to address emotional, spiritual, and sometimes physical issues.

Vision and clarity: The process of defining your financial and life goals with precision and understanding your nonnegotiables—those elements that you are not willing to compromise on.

Nonnegotiables: Firm boundaries or standards that you set for yourself, particularly in your financial life. These are the principles that guide your decisions and actions.

Divorcing your old financial self: The metaphorical process of letting go of outdated financial habits, beliefs, and identities that no longer serve your best interests. It's about transforming into a new financial identity aligned with your goals.

Big-picture thinking: The ability to focus on long-term goals and outcomes rather than getting bogged down by day-to-day challenges. It involves maintaining perspective and staying aligned with your overall vision.

Conscious redesign: The deliberate process of restructuring your financial life to align with your goals, values, and desires. It's about making intentional decisions that support your vision for the future.

Three-account system: A money management strategy that involves dividing your finances into three separate accounts for operating (daily expenses), saving, and enjoying (fun or discretionary spending). This system helps to simplify financial management and reduce stress.

Financial inventory: Similar to the term used in Break the Glass Ceiling, it's a comprehensive review of your finances, often used as the first step in the conscious redesign process.

Spending account: An account specifically designated for discretionary spending, allowing you to enjoy your money guilt free while keeping other financial goals on track.

Automating savings: The practice of setting up automatic transfers from your checking account to your savings account, ensuring that you consistently save without having to think about it.

Investing trifecta: The three ways to invest: time, people, and money. It's about understanding that financial success is linked not just to monetary investments but also to how you spend your time and who you surround yourself with.

Financial forecasting: The process of projecting your financial situation into the future, often using tools like a twelve-month financial tracker. It helps you plan for long-term goals and anticipate potential challenges.

REFERENCES

American Psychological Association. "The Impact of Money on Mental Health: A Comprehensive Study," 2020.

Brown, Brené. *Daring Greatly: How the Courage to Be Vulnerable Transforms the Way We Live, Love, Parent, and Lead.* Avery, 2012.

Chastain, Lisa, host. *Real Money.* Podcast. "Former Tony Robbins CFO Hits Rock Bottom and Provides Great Advice to Come Back." March 5, 2024. https://lisachastain.com/former-tony-robbins-cfo-hits-rock-bottom-and-provides-great-advice-to-come-back/.

Chastain, Lisa, host. *Real Money.* Podcast. "Energy Healing and Money with Rosalyn Acosta." July 18, 2024. https://lisachastain.com/energy-healing-and-money-with-rosalyn-acosta/.

Duhigg, Charles. *The Power of Habit: Why We Do What We Do in Life and Business.* Random House, 2014.

Hoover, Joy. "Empowering Women Through Beauty and Safety." Esoes Cosmetics. 2024.

Morrison, Toni. *Beloved*. Alfred A. Knopf, 1993.

Robbins, Tony. *Awaken the Giant Within: How to Take Immediate Control of Your Mental, Emotional, Physical, and Financial Destiny!* Free Press, 1992.

U.S. Bank. "Women and Wealth Insights Study." 2020. https://www.usbank.com/dam/documents/pdf/wealth-management/perspectives/women-and-wealth-insights-study_07-2020.pdf.

ABOUT THE AUTHOR

As a graduate of the University of Nevada, Las Vegas, Lisa Chastain brings over twenty years of experience empowering women to take control of their financial futures. From her roles as an academic adviser in higher education to serving as a financial adviser for high-net-worth individuals, Chastain's journey has led to her current role as a money coach for women seeking financial health.

Photo by Casey Jade

Chastain's qualifications extend beyond professional experience; she has navigated her own financial challenges, learning firsthand what it takes to rebuild and thrive. Leaving behind a safe and stable career in 2016, she transitioned to become a personal finance coach, driven by a passion to help women shed shame and guilt around money.

Through her strategic financial framework focused on healthy spending, she helped clients rewrite their money narratives and achieve financial freedom. Chastain's journey from financial failure to success has been featured in CNBC, NBC News, *O, The Oprah Magazine*, and more. As a bestselling author and host of the *Real Money* podcast, Chastain is dedicated to empowering women to live their best lives, free from financial stress and worry.